CW01064333

THE VINCENT BLACK SHADOW

Tim Kingham

AMBERLEY

Front cover: A great example of a Vincent Black Shadow capable of being used on today's roads while retaining all the basic qualities of yesterday's motorcycles. (Photo by Bob Southall)

First published 2017

Amberley Publishing
The Hill, Stroud
Gloucestershire, GL5 4EP

www.amberley-books.com

Copyright © Tim Kingham, 2017

The right of Tim Kingham to be identified as the Author of this work has been asserted in accordance with the Copyrights, Designs and Patents Act 1988.

ISBN 978 1 4456 6722 5 (print)
ISBN 978 1 4456 6723 2 (ebook)

All rights reserved. No part of this book may be reprinted or reproduced or utilised in any form or by any electronic, mechanical or other means, now known or hereafter invented, including photocopying and recording, or in any information storage or retrieval system, without the permission in writing from the Publishers.

British Library Cataloguing in Publication Data.
A catalogue record for this book is available from the British Library.

Origination by Amberley Publishing.
Printed in the UK.

Contents

Acknowledgements

The board and staff of the VOC Spares Company Ltd (Vincent Spares).

The executive and assistants of the Vincent Owners HRD Club, in particular: Richard Wheeldon – ex-director Vincent Spares and VOC ex-Liaison officer; Marcus Bowden – VOC overseas representative; Paul Adams – VOC information officer; Peter Bell – VOC club archivist; Simon Dinsdale – VOC machine registrar; and Tony Milbourn – VOC Spares liaison officer.

VOC Members in particular: Andy Glasgow; Ben Kingham BSKSpeedworks; Eddie Grew; Geoff Preece; Jenny Bloor; Norman Walker; Bob Southall; and Rob Staley.

My dear wife Angela, for checking the text and taking pictures.

Ian Savage – managing director of Vincent Spares – for checking technical details and text.

My Vincents for keeping running, even after I neglected them in writing this book.

Foreword

When Tim Kingham asked me to write a foreword for his new book on the Vincent Black Shadow, I thought 'do we need another Vincent book?', but looking along the bookshelf I realised most of the books we refer to regularly are out of print, so how is the new or prospective owner to get the right information – the Internet? We all know that what passes for collective knowledge on the web can be at least misleading or at worst just plain wrong. Now is the perfect time for a new volume.

Tim's well-researched work gives the new or aspiring owner and old hand equally a first-class source of information, including insights into the workings of the Vincent company, Vincent HRD Owners Club, modifiers, racers, suppliers and, most importantly, riders of Vincent machines in general, and Black Shadows in particular.

You may notice in the list above I didn't mention investors. Many will say the status of the Black Shadow as the 'must have' investment machine is a bad thing. I'll leave you to debate that. What it does mean is that a relatively minor matter, to a rider, can greatly affect the value of a Black Shadow. Is 'value' the correct word? Maybe 'price' is better. We know the value of a Vincent is derived from riding it.

Knowledge is king and invaluable and this book provides it in bucketfulls!

Ian Savage
Vincent Owner
MD of the VOC Spares Co. Ltd

CHAPTER ONE

The Legend

Confusion Unbounded

The heading on the Vincent HRD Owners Club (VOC) website proudly proclaims 'Home of the Legendary Black Shadow', and that pride is undoubtedly justified. Unfortunately, when looking up the word 'legend' in dictionaries, a sentence often encountered in its description is 'not necessarily authenticated'. It is common knowledge that anyone who knows anything about motorcycles has heard something about the fabled beast. Yet people, even journalists, who claim to be interested in motorcycles, often assume, or are at least complicit in continuing the myth, that all Vincent twins are Black Shadows. In turn it is not unknown for an owner to imply that his Vincent is a Black Shadow when it is not.

There is also the vast amount of misinformation to be found when enquiring on the subject. Obviously, at the technical and enthusiast level, there are some books that the knowledgeable soon put on their reading list; to give just two examples, *Vincent Motorcycles* by Jacqueline Bickerstaff and *Know thy Beast* by Eddie Stevens. These deal in accurate minute technical detail with all Vincent machines and are excellent references to the original machine. When one looks at the wider media, however, confusion and misrepresentation reign supreme. Songs and poems have been penned, tin plaques with distorted images and inappropriate texts have been manufactured, T-shirts and mugs have been made with reversed images, and newspaper articles and mainstream fictional books have been written, all full of information that is incorrect. As well as these, spoof articles are to be found on the Internet. There is one about a non-existent model – 'The Black Widow' – and another tall story about Royal Enfield's parent Indian company buying the Vincent name. All this misinformation just adds to the confusion.

One supposes none of this would have occurred if the Black Shadow had been an ordinary bike with ordinary performance, with a name consisting of numbers and letters. Remember also, it first appeared in an era of post-war austerity and drabness, with a performance that at that time was far ahead of anything else on the roads of the world. This meant the Vincent company's famous strap line 'The worlds fastest standard motorcycle' was not only true, but remained true – so much so that it soon occupied a niche in the public consciousness that has endured ever since. One cannot blame poets, composers, advertisers and writers for associating their heroes and products with such an iconic machine; it is just a pity they could not check their details while they were in pursuit of the legend.

Reasons for Confusion

When one considers the growth of the legend and the confusion surrounding the Black Shadow, there are a number of primary factors that come to mind. The first is the closeness in specification between the three post-war Vincent twins. The three were the original Rapide, the subsequent sports version developed from it (the actual Black Shadow), and the further development – the racing version called the Black Lightning. We shall explore in particular the differences between the Rapide and the Black Shadow later, but the bald fact we had better get in the open straight away is that there really is little difference between the Rapide and the Black Shadow, especially after the passage of seventy years.

This brings us to the second factor adding confusion. Most of the Vincent was made on normal engineering equipment, which was found in any factory in the mid-twentieth century. Most of the parts that differentiated the models were made with processes that are easily copied and emulated to a point where the 10-horsepower difference between, say, a Black Shadow and a Rapide was soon eliminated. It is also a fact that many of the Vincent owners were and still are from technical or mechanical backgrounds and are thus able to produce components and modifications with relative ease. In the first two or three decades after production commenced, many of these owners often proceeded to campaign their steeds in competition on road and track to the point of destruction; often swapping engines and frames with wild abandon. These are all factors that combine to increase the difficulties in untangling the legend.

The final factor to be considered is the situation and actions of the factory itself. Production after the war was nothing like the computerised and automated process we have today. Now, so many of the components are made by subcontractors to rigid specifications, who are tied by legislation and driven by compromises forged by the manufacturers competing departments in endless meetings. Vincent's small factory was located in Old Stevenage, in existing buildings that now house a school. Most of the machined parts were made there initially on machinery that had been through the war producing aircraft components and bomb fuses and were not necessarily specialised for motorcycle production. Although further premises were obtained a small distance away[1], a lot of the component manufacture, the assembly work from wheel building, engine and machine assembly, plus painting and engine testing, were initially done on the original site, while the road testing was carried out on the public roads.[2] The entire organisation was under the direct and immediate control of Philip Conrad Vincent (PCV) himself, with a small board of directors.

The sales field consisted of a small circle of distributors and overseas agents who passed orders to the factory, but it was not unusual for the factory to receive direct requests from customers. Changes were incorporated, as they were deemed necessary either by way of improvements, customer feedback, or shortages of raw materials and components. Those personnel that carried out assembly of the bikes were known as 'fitters', because it was a job that was not a simple assembly exercise since a certain amount of skill and remedial work was required to assemble (fit) the parts. As has been already pointed out, at one time the factory was producing three similar twin cylinder models. Unlike the built-in obsolescence and 'not user serviceable' policies that bedevils products of today, most upgrades were backward compatible to earlier machines and could be easily retrofitted, so not only was there a background of development changes,

A view of the Vincent factory yard in Old Stevenage. (Photo by Geoff Preece)

most of the defining components for the models were interchangeable. This is one of the reasons the particular year when a Vincent was built has little influence on its price. Often the factory itself took advantage of this interchangeability to 'retro fit' upgrades to customer's machines, to repair, and even to swap engines and frames. They were also ready to pander to customers or dealers' specific requests for touring or performance parts; a good example of this policy is the Black Shadow's black engine paint, which is the most obvious departure from a standard Rapide, and even that was not sacrosanct. A number of 'White Shadows' were also produced identical to the current Black Shadows, but without the black-painted engines. To further confuse the issue, one of those was part of a consignment supplied in Chinese-red paintwork! Overarching all those factors that can cause confusion, it is also important to remember the financial status of the company was frequently perilous and a desperate company is more interested in getting machines out of the door rather than being pernickety about uniformity.

The Real Black Shadow

All the above raises the question, when is a motorcycle claiming to be a Black Shadow a real Black Shadow? Most of the modifications introduced by the factory to produce the

Black Shadow sports model were developed with much effort on the dynamometer in the engine shed at Stevenage, on the A1 road in the early morning and on the primitive post-war airfields of Bedfordshire. The items that resulted from this development work have now been available for decades in replica form to anyone who has a little research time and some money. The term 'Shadow Spec' is well ingrained in the Vincent aficionado's vocabulary and many Rapides are now adorned with a specification that equals, or exceeds, the original Black Shadow specification. For appreciation of its design and its line, a reasonable rule is if a motorcycle looks acceptable from 5 feet away then generally it is. There is one problem with applying that rule rigidly: you cannot see frame or engine numbers from 5 feet away.

Does the answer then rely on a couple of punched letters on the engine or frame? If it has that mark then it is a Black Shadow. Well, to be strictly correct, to the collector what marks are on the crankcase certainly do matter. Also important is the relationship between the frame number and the engine number. In most but not all cases, there is a rule followed by the factory in their allocation of those numbers, but that is only a rule of thumb. More importantly, collectors need to know they are the numbers that match the factory records. When they are satisfied it meets their conditions, it seems collectors are willing to pay. At the time of writing one can expect a Black Shadow to command some 80 to 100 per cent, or more, in value than a Rapide in similar condition. It has to be an exceptional Rapide to be worth more than a basket case Black Shadow. For the owner who is a rider and not a collector or speculator, it really makes little difference what his model is; it is nice to have an original machine, but not essential as he still has a fine bike to ride, which is not going to depreciate. For him the '5 foot rule' is perfectly acceptable. If there is one attribute that characterises the Vincent owner from the fifties until now, it is the desire to improve what was already an exceedingly good machine; just as Rapide owners 'Shadowised' their steeds, Black Shadow owners 'improved' and often 'Lightningised' theirs.

So there we have it – three closely specified models from a factory bending to commercial pressures, open to component availability and specification upgrades, followed by sixty years of owners busily modifying and 'improving' their machines. Add a layer of misinformation and exaggeration and it should be no surprise that an extant perfect Black Shadow, with an appropriate performance attached, is almost as difficult to capture as the second part of its name suggests.

CHAPTER TWO

Birth of a New Machine

The Vincent Company

Like most legends the Black Shadow was not created overnight. PCV had bought the defunct HRD firm in 1928 after persuading his father to invest in his dream of manufacturing motorcycles. HRD were the initials of Howard Raymond Davis, who had won a TT on his own built machine. Since HRD had been an idol of PCV, it seemed a good place to start with a company that had a recognised name; badge engineering, it seems, was not new even in 1928! Eight years later, after using a variety of proprietary engines in his machines, PCV had in 1936 metamorphosed (some say by a breath of wind turning a tracing over on a drawing board) the 500 Series 'A', powered by their own built single cylinder engine, into a vee twin with great potential, but with an Achilles heel of a proprietary clutch and, to some extent, a gearbox that could not handle the power.

Then came the Second World War, when motorcycle production ceased but not the designer's imagination. From as early as November 1943, *The Motorcycle* published a number of Vincent patents under the title 'A trend for thought'. In March 1945 *The Motorcycle* published a page about a revised Series 'A' twin, where most of the new features were discussed in the article headed 'A 400lb 998 cc big twin!' Although the article had only a single photograph of the pre-war twin, there was no doubt that a market existed for an updated big twin because letters soon started to arrive at the factory requesting details of when motorcycle production would be resumed. A brochure was issued in April 1945 and by late 1945 the demand was being answered by letters explaining that the enquirers name would be added to a list and they would be contacted when production started. Based on, but fully differentiated from, the pre-war models, it was also designated as the 'Series B' Rapide, but post-war shortages of material thwarted even the development programme, let alone production. A year later, in September 1946, production of the standard Series 'B' Rapide finally started. It was a slow start and for the rest of 1946 only nineteen bikes were produced. The slogan 'Export or Die' was at that time very near the truth, as of those nineteen produced, only seven remained in the UK.[3]

Two people are always associated with the design of the Vincent twins – PCV and Phil Irving, commonly known as 'the two Phils'. When one reads their respective biographies, it is sometimes difficult to untangle who designed what and when; indeed, at some points the narratives often contradict each other. Obviously PCV was the driving force and it is convenient to name him in the story, however Phil Irving should not be ignored. He was a remarkable designer from Australia, who had two periods of work at Vincents and Velocette, before leaving in 1949 to continue his design career back in Australia with, among others, EMC and Formula One winner Repco Brabham.

Above: Howard Raymond Davis after his senior win in the 1925 TT on his company's HRD. (Image supplied by Stilltime Collection www.stilltimecollection.co.uk)

Right: This sales brochure dating from April 1945 was issued more than three years before the motorcycle was in production. Inside it suggested that interested buyers should get their name entered onto the firm's 'interested' list. The specification of the proposed engine and transmission were described in some detail, while those of the frame were a little sketchy. However, it was indicated that the Series 'A' rear suspension system would be retained. (Tim Kingham collection)

Advance details of our

POST-WAR

" Rapide " Motor-Cycle

HRD

The Vincent H.R.D. Company Ltd.
Stevenage,
Herts.

APRIL, 1945.

Telephone & Telegrams :   ON WAR OFFICE &   Code :
Stevenage 375 (2 Lines)   AIR MINISTRY LISTS   A.B.C. 7th Edition.

The VINCENT COMPANY Ltd.

PRECISION ENGINEERS

MAKERS OF : VINCENT H.R.D. MOTOR CYCLES :
MARINE & INDUSTRIAL ENGINES : "RAPIDE" JIGS, TOOLS & GAUGES

STEVENAGE
HERTS.

Our Ref........HKM/KMB........

Your Ref........................

1st. December 1945

Capt. ███████████████.
79th. Medium Regt. R.A.(Scottish Horse) T.A.
B.A.O.R.

Dear Sir,

    We thank you for your letter of the 28th.October which we
have perused with some considerable interest.

    We take this opportunity of enclosing for your immediate
information, advance literature relating to our 1946 production,the
Series " B " Rapide. Your perusal of this literature coupled with
the very full technical description with photographs and drawings,
that will be appearing in the technical press in the near future,
will, I am sure, provide the answers to a number of the queries
raised in your letter.

    We at all times appreciate receiving letters dealing in
technicalities from members of the motorcycling fraternity and from
time to time have pleasure in welcoming such members at our Stevenage
Works. Should you, at some later date, be able to avail yourself of
the invitation that we now have pleasure in extending to you, to
visit us and see for yourself the excellent quality of material and
workmanship that goes into our productions, we shall be delighted to
discuss with you any technical details that you may care to raise.

    As we have for some time past been inundated with orders
both from this Country and overseas, we have instituted a rotation
system whereby prospective purchasers may assure themselves of de-
liveries in strict datal order. The placing of clients names on this
list incurs no legal obligation but assures the purchaser of the
delivery of his machine at a date earlier than he would obtain by
waiting to place his initial order.

                                                    (cont'd over)

This is a letter that accompanied the later brochure – naturally many of the prospective customers were serving in the forces. It does appear to be in response to a letter sent to the company expressing interest in the new machine. (Tim Kingham collection)

(cont'd)

    We trust that we shall have the pleasure of hearing from
you again in the immediate future and shall, on receipt of any advice from you, have pleasure in entering your name on the aforesaid
rotation list.

    Thanking you for the very real interest you have displayed
in our production and assuring you of our best attention at all times.

                        Yours faithfully,
            For. THE VINCENT H.R.D. COMPANY LTD.

                        Mainwa...

                        Sales Department.

The reverse of the above letter. The signature looks like that of Mr Mainwaring, the Vincent Sales Manager. It is worth noting that this letter is not a duplicate and shows the way in which customers could expect to be treated if they revealed an interest in what was a very exclusive product. (Tim Kingham collection)

This is a later ten-paged brochure dated around the end of 1945, noted as the 7th edition, but prepared earlier in that year. The only photo-illustration was inside and was of a Series 'A', but the text made it clear that the new bike was to be called the Series 'B' Rapide. The artist's impression of the new Series 'B' as a race bike complete with rider was repeated inside. The text also stated performance as 110 mph in top. (Tim Kingham collection)

This is the detailed drawing of the engine unit from the 1945 brochure; it is remarkably like the final product that appeared almost two years later, making it an interesting exercise to see what changes occurred between the original drawing and the final product. (Tim Kingham collection)

The Series 'B' Rapide in production; the triangular stand in the foreground probably supported the RFM and engine while the UFM was fitted. (Picture courtesy of the Vincent HRD Owners Club)

The Rapide

The bike was a revolution in design. Once in production it was the basis of the Black Shadow and its racing counterpart, the Black Lightning, which was later derived from it. Since any examination of the Black Shadow cannot ignore its sister and precursor, the Rapide, what follows is an examination of and concentration on the unique features of the original Series 'B' Rapide that are common to all the Vincent twins, and directly to the Series 'B' Black Shadow. Perhaps it may help to allay the once prevalent complaint that the Vincent is a collection of engineering solutions looking for a problem.

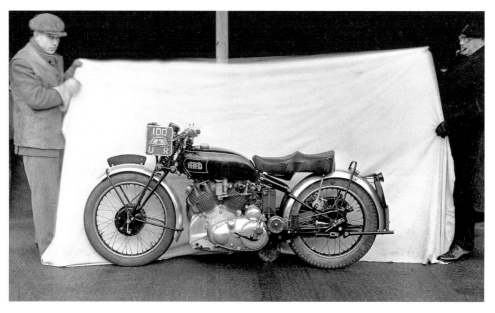

Above: An early Series 'B' Rapide, probably just before its first road test. The trade plate obscures the headlamp. Petrol was available for commercial use, which included road tests. (Image supplied by Stilltime Collection www.stilltimecollection.co.uk)

Below: The Rapide road test. Charles Markham testing the then new Series 'B' Rapide and getting 'well down to it'. (Image supplied by Stilltime Collection www.stilltimecollection.co.uk)

Another view of the road test. The background gives a good illustration of the conditions in which most machines were tested. Vincent's test track was the old A1 (The Great North Road); apart from the 30 mph limit in towns there were no speed restrictions. (Image supplied by Stilltime Collection www.stilltimecollection.co.uk)

The Engine

The engine was an all-alloy 50 degree 84 mm by 90 mm vee-twin engine, which followed the pre-war design, but while the bore and stroke remained the same as the pre-war Series 'A', the angle between the cylinders was altered to a 50 degree configuration rather than the pre-war 47.5 degrees. This was to allow the use of a standard Lucas magneto. This still meant a compromise because a standard magneto does not perform at its electrical best on a vee-twin, since its optimum flux is obtained at 180 degrees of rotation. To amend this defect, platinum points were originally specified for the magneto. Although the angle of the vee-twin was altered from the pre-war model, the unique twin valve guide arrangement with the valve actuated from the middle by stiff rockers situated in the tunnels in the head was retained, which undoubtedly provided a longer life for the valve and a cooler life for the now coil valve springs. The shortened pushrod length and the substantial valve gear allowed the engine to rev higher than might be expected from its dimensions. The compression ratio was by modern standards extremely low and was supplied with a compression plate to bring it below 6.5:1, which was necessitated by the pool petrol, which was all that was available at the time. Specialoid pistons were used. The barrels were deeply sunk into the crankcase with spigotted heads with interlocking ground faces that needed no head gasket. The cylinders were slightly offset to aid cooling and also to accommodate the side-by-side big end arrangement. The rotating and reciprocating oil pump was driven via a worm gear on the right-hand end of the crankshaft. The oil was distributed via passages in the timing cover to the cams and the bottom end, while the return line supplied the rockers.

The arrangement of the valve gear. The valve guides are situated above and below the rocker actuation point. The rocker action is transmitted to the shoulder of the wider lower valve stem by a removable collar. The small collets that retain the valve are at the top and are secured by a small spring in a groove in the valve stem. They should always be bought as a machined pair. The ET100 bolt shown, which secures the rocker bearing in its tunnel, is the standard design. The relative shortness of the pushrod can also be seen. (Photo by Tim Kingham)

The Transmission

With the less than optimum performance in the pre-war twin of the Burman clutch, and with some doubts about whether the separate gearbox from the same manufacturer would be able to handle the proposed power, PCV decided that he would manufacture his own clutch and gearbox. This would fit into a box that was part of the engine casting, thus forming a unit construction engine. This seemed a logical decision, however a rather more controversial choice was to design the gearbox as a crossover box. The drive entered on the left via a triplex primary chain and exited on the right, necessitated by virtue of the fact that the clutch was in a separate chamber to avoid the primary drive oil, and a final drive sprocket on that side would make the unit too wide. At the time a crossover box was fairly unconventional thinking, but the massive walls of the unit construction engine casting was found in practice to have eliminated any possible twisting problems that this type of layout may have produced in a separate gearbox and engine layout. Indeed, this crossover configuration has never proved a problem. The gearbox itself comprised very strong gears manufactured in EN36 steel. Movement of the gears was actuated by a horizontally mounted selector disc above the gear cluster that contained the selector fork guide paths driven by a bevel drive from the selector arm. This arm included an external extension to aid selection of neutral by hand and to indicate the gear selected. The selection mechanism gear change, lever shaft and kick-start were housed in a stress-free cover that fastened on to the load-bearing gearbox plate that was itself fixed to the engine casting.

There is an often heard comment that the Vincent clutch is a centrifugal clutch and a cursory examination might suggest this is correct; it does in fact owe more in design

A top down view of a new twin crankcase. The picture is centred on the rear cylinder opening and shows the strong unit construction casting and gearbox section. The small hole in the top centre of the picture is the gearbox filler hole. (Photo courtesy of Vincent Spares)

A view of the gearbox internals in the Vincent spares checking jig. It was taken from the rear of the assembly and shows the position of the cam plate over the top of gear cluster. The mainshaft clutch end is on the left and the tips of the final drive sprocket are just visible between the right-hand jig wall and the aluminium gearbox endplate. (Photo courtesy of Vincent Spares)

to a drum brake in reverse and this is perhaps the easiest way to picture it. In this imaginary drum brake, each of the shoes is leading and has one end pivoted and one end free, which is connected by a link to the central mechanism. The clutch operates in the following way: once the clutch lever is released, power is transmitted from the outer drum via a small single friction driving plate to the central mechanism by a U section ring. The attached shoes are pushed out and, by virtue of the two links then being almost over centre, they wedge themselves against the drum and remain there transmitting power until the clutch lever is pulled in. This causes the driving plate to be lifted, the friction plate to loose its grip, and the shoes to fall back from the drum.

There is a little more to it than that; springs, plungers and toggle links all combine to make it one of the lightest clutches ever likely to be found, yet still capable of transmitting a great deal of power. In fact, the spring pressure on the single driving plate was increased simply to give a better feeling of control on the lever when

The Vincent clutch internals showing the clutch drum with the shoes in place around the central spring holder. On the top right is a later one-piece friction plate that provides the thrust via a clutch plate (not shown) to the drum. On the left is a separate single shoe in the centre of which can be seen the sprung plunger, while the hole for the link pivot can be seen on the top of the link. (Photo by Tim Kingham)

operating. The one problem that stalked the design, apart from its complexity, was the fact that it needed to be kept oil free. As already mentioned, to aid this, the clutch was situated in its own chamber separated from the primary drive and isolated by oil seals, and in turn, this necessitated a rather wide engine at that point. Final drive was by $^{3/8}$ inch by $^{5/16}$ inch chain, which ran over a standard rear sprocket of forty-eight teeth. The resultant gearing allowed 4,600 rpm of the engine to correspond to a road speed of 100 mph.

The Frame and Suspension

PCV also wanted to keep the wheelbase comparable with sporting 500 cc motorcycles of the period. This desire was aided by the early decision to employ unit construction to strengthen the gearbox and transmission. His aim was to get the wheelbase down to 56 inches, which was over 2 inches shorter than the Series 'A'. Bearing in mind that the pre-war twin had a narrower vee configuration than the new engine, this was indeed a tall order. A full-scale drawing of the proposed machine soon made it clear that employing a tubular frame similar to the Series 'A' did not achieve this goal and indeed it was seen that the front wheel clearances to the front down tube would make this impossible. However, his true genius was proved when he achieved his goal by simply removing the frame and using the massive unit construction engine as the frame member. This unit was suspended from an assembly of a headstock forging and fabricated oil tank, known in the Vincent world as the UFM (Upper Frame Member), which connected on to two forgings mounted on the heads of the two cylinders. The rear suspension – known in the Vincent world as the RFM (Rear

Frame Member) – was a feature that actually predated the Vincent HRD Company, because PCV had introduced it on the first bike he designed back in 1927.[4] During the pre-war years, however, in spite of it being used on the Series 'A' machines, much of the buying public was not in favour of sprung frames. One minor advantage of this

Bare UFM with head cup bearings inserted. The attachment points at the left end are (top to bottom) seat pivot, spring and damper mounting, and sidecar attachment point. On the underside further towards the right is the slotted rear cylinder attachment point and even further to the right is the front cylinder mounting point. (Photo courtesy of BSK Speedworks)

The RFM with pivot bearings in place with brake crossover spindle and brake arms fitted. The seat support arms together with damper assemblies have also been attached. Damper and spring boxes await assembly. (Photo courtesy of BSK Speedworks)

design back then was that it tended to hide the fact the machine had rear springing; however, by the late forties the tide was turning with bikes like the Douglas starting to appear with rear springing. PCV felt his RFM was superior to the other alternative rear springing designs because of its proven essential rigidity and its success in the Series 'A' machines. So, after rearranging the taper roller bearings within the structure and carrying out a few other minor changes, he incorporated it into the new machine. The only real criticism levelled against the Vincent RFM was its unsprung weight, but it should be remembered that only a proportion of the weight is in movement, because in operation the mass around the pivot oscillates only a small amount. Meanwhile, after a few years of flirtation with compromise solutions, like plunger rear ends, sprung hubs, and wear-prone Ansty links, the rest of the industry slowly went over to various renditions of the swinging arm concept. PCV's unique solution to rear suspension remained a solitary example until Yamaha 'invented' it in 1973 on their Monoshock off-road motorcycle.

The next ground-breaking innovation was the inclusion of a dual seat. This was not the first iteration of the idea, since Velocette had fitted a dual seat to the 1934 TT works racers named by the inimitable Harold Willis as the *Loch Ness Monster*. While that Velocette was a rigid machine and also a racer, here on the road-going Vincent PCV had to incorporate his dual seat with the RFM in motion underneath, while also avoiding the high seat position so prevalent nowadays, but an anathema back then. His solution was to pivot the seat at the front by attaching it by a spindle to the UFM, and supporting it at the rear by hinged stays attached to the lower ends of the RFM. Thus, the rear of the seat (the pillion) moves as a fraction of the rear wheel movement, while the front (the rider) hardly alters position. Inclusion in the rear seat stays of two friction dampers allowed the movement of the seat to be controlled dependant on load and conditions by a few turns of the adjusting knobs.

At the front end, for reasons of design capacity and material availability, PCV decided to stay with the tried and tested Brampton forks as used with the Series 'A'. PCV did not wish to join the headlong rush to the telescopic fork, which he considered a poor engineering solution. He disliked the excessive dip under heavy braking and the fact its legs were prone to twist and deform. Its sole advantage, he felt, which had been developed during the war, was the extended springs for off-road use, and he also thought it was important to get the new model into production, so he decided any new fork solution would have to wait. However, he did make some alterations in the Brampton's geometry and also placed 'Oilite' bushes in the spindle housings. On top of the forks, the handlebars were of the type still sold in today's motorcycle shops, known as 'Vincent straights', although higher touring bars were available.

A lot of thought went into the provision of adjustable controls. In particular, the rider's footrests were folding; this is an innovation that is welcome in a tight garage and a feature that the single 500 cc Comet owners are immensely envious of – perhaps more than their missing rear cylinder. These folding footrests hung down from the engine, the left-hand side contained the brake lever, while the right-hand contained the gear change lever. Thus, movement of the footrests forward or backward did not change the position of the operating pedals relative to the pivot. A further innovation was that both the gear change pedal and the footbrake pedal had been designed so they both could be reversed, if wished, which meant they could be operated from the pillion footrest position. This feature pointed towards the sporting potential of the Rapide and the possibility of a future sports model.

A view of an early Series 'B' engine, showing the early gear change arrangement. Very few of these were fitted to Black Shadows as wear soon developed in the linkages. (Photo supplied by Mortons Media Archive)

A view of the left-hand footrest and brake lever. The alternative rearward cable outer boss can be seen on the leg. If the footrest itself was removed and the brake arm reversed, the brake could be operated from the pillion footrest. (Photo courtesy of BSK Speedworks)

The front and back mudguards were made in aluminium of a type called 'Birmabright'. It is believed to be the same type of high-quality alloy used in Land Rovers of the same era. From 1948 touring types could also avail themselves of steel guards of a more enveloping nature. The rear stand remained of a pre-war design, substantial and secured to the rear mudguard flap, pivoting at the rear of the machine. There was a quoted technique for operating it, but once down it was very effective. A lot of thought and ingenuity went into the front stand, situated under the magneto and oil chamber on two plates at the front of the engine. Each side contained a prop stand that individually swung out to prop up either side of the machine as required. The really clever part was with both stand legs in the folded closed position, loosening of the front aluminium cowl and removal of a single bolt allowing the complete assembly to be rotated down under spring pressure and thus provide two legs of a front stand that would support the front wheel clear of the ground for puncture repairs. In addition, after the removal of the tank, head lug bolts, and the uncoupling of some

Timing side view of a Black Shadow fitted with the alternative steel touring guards. The stoplight switch near the rear wheel spindle is rectangular, while very early ones were round. (Photo courtesy of Andrew Glasgow)

Drive side view of the touring Black Shadow; the handlebars are to the more upright touring design. Small box on top of dynamo is shape of the original Miller regulator. (Photo courtesy of Andrew Glasgow)

wiring plugs and cables, it allowed the whole front of the machine, comprising the front wheel, headlamp, forks, controls and oil tank, to be removed from the bike and wheeled away in one piece. This left the engine transmission and rear wheel assemblies standing proudly on the workshop floor ready for servicing. Truly with a Vincent, the frame is taken off the engine, not the engine out of the frame.

Above: The left-hand front side stand in position while the opposite stand remains folded. (Note extra pad on bottom of foot) (Photo by Bob Southall)

Right: Removing one bolt enables both folded front stands to be rotated down and then the whole machine can be pulled backwards, forming a front stand that leaves the front wheel clear of the ground. (Photo by Bob Southall)

Wheels and Brakes

The wheels were still basically of a pre-war design with nothing unusual about the individual brakes, which were very similar to the Series 'A'. These consisted of two alloy shoes 7/8 inch wide set in a 7-inch drum, initially of steel (changed to cast iron in 1947). What was exceptional in contemporary terms was that there were four drums on the bike. Each wheel comprised of an alloy 'cotton reel' with two separate spoke flanges and with drums, disposed equally each side of the centre line and running on taper roller bearings. This design was applied to front and rear wheels with only detailed changes. All brakes had a steel brake plate and were soon enhanced by an alloy water shield.

At the rear, as noted in the transmission description, the standard sprocket was of forty-eight teeth mounted on the periphery of the brake drum. To vary the final drive ratio for sidecar and other situations, the sprocket size could be varied between forty-six and fifty-six teeth (nominally). It should be noted that because of the mirror image profile of the wheel, the rear wheel could be reversed to bring an alternative sprocket, if fitted, into use. The twin torque arms were retained by spring-loaded clips, which engaged in a grooved post. This, coupled with knurled hand click chain adjusters, pull out trunnions, a lift up mudguard flap, and a rear spindle complete with a captive nut and tommy bar, meant the wheel could be removed without the use of any tools. Some claimed it still needed a set of pliers to undo the chain, but with thought it could be artfully festooned around the RFM in one piece and the wheel slipped out.

Front brake water shields riveted to the steel brake plate; those shown are stainless steel, but the original shields would have been in aluminium. (Photo courtesy of BSK Speedworks)

Twin sprockets fitted to a rear wheel. The wheel hub is symmetrical and thus it can be reversed to present an alternative sprocket. (Photo by Angela Kingham)

Close-up of the rear wheel. The spring clip on the brake anchor arm can be seen behind the rear stand leg. The tommy bar on the wheel spindle is above it and the adjustment serrations on the brake arm are in the top right of the picture. The left-hand knurled adjuster for the wheel can be just seen behind the tommy bar. (Photo by Angela Kingham)

Wheel size was a 19-inch WM2 with an 18-inch WM3 as the touring alternative. The twin brakes were operated by twin rods pivoted on the swinging arm, which in turn were actuated by a short cable, thus completely isolating the pedal from rear fork movement. The standard rear wheel was shod with an Avon studded 3.50 x 19 'Supreme'.

On the front wheel, the right-hand plate was provided with a hole to locate a right-angle drive speedometer drive assembly, which ran off an internal hub mounted cog. The front spindle was provided with a tommy bar and captive nut. The brake operating arms were multi-adjustable in very small increments by use of a serrated washer with over twenty radial grooves and a matching grooved lever, with an offset

Front brake balance beam. The brake cable descends on the left-hand side of the bike and after locating on the beam continues down to the left-hand brake arm; the other end of the beam pulls on a shorter right-hand slave cable. This bike has the later modification 'V' support fitted. The beam limit stop is the slotted head pin under the arm on the right-hand side of the bike. (Photo by Angela Kingham)

square hole, which fitted on the brake cam spindle. This fully adjustable method was also used on the rear wheel. Front wheel size was a 20-inch WM1 rim and a 19-inch WM2 as the touring alternative. The front brake operation was developed from the pre-war design and was operated by a single cable to a pivoted beam, mounted on the fork that equalised the pull to both brakes; again, the wheel could be removed without tools. The standard wheel was fitted with an Avon ribbed 3.00 x 20 'Speedster'.

Electrics

Miller supplied the lights and electrical equipment. The specification was perhaps the best available at the time, being 6 Volts with an 8-inch headlight, together with a 3.5-inch-diameter dynamo and a 13-Amp hour battery. This offering from the industry did little to ensure the machine could be used at night. Its collection of components was in all a combination produced for many other contemporary machines. It is worth

The Miller pattern STOP light. The bottom half of the lens is the rear light, the top half is the stop light. A clear panel on the bottom side illuminates the number plate. (Photo courtesy of Vincent Spares)

noting the characteristic small rear light with the word STOP in metal silhouette on the red lens, although often called a Vincent stoplight, is not in fact exclusive to Vincent, since there are other pre- and post-war motorcycles that also used this Miller offering. Although many were removed during the sixties and replaced with Lucas 564, or similar rear lights, it has now been retrofitted to many Vincents, but it really is not an adequate rear light and, if fitted, needs some modification. During 1948 the headlamp size was reduced to what was commonly referred to as the 6 and a half inch size.

Finish

The machine's forks, rear frame, tanks, and small steel parts were painted in black, which set it off from the aluminium mudguards and engine.[5] There was little chrome employed, which was mostly on proprietary parts, but a surprising amount of stainless steel was used instead. Fixings and fastenings not in stainless steel were cadmium plated.

Chapter Three

The Black Shadow Emerges

Gunga Din

During the early summer of 1947 the factory production of Rapides was increasing and George Brown, who had been with the Vincent HRD Company since before the war, and already an acknowledged racer of Series 'A' Vincent twins and singles, became eager to try the new twin in competition. So, helped by Phil Irving and George's brother Cliff, they started to develop a factory hack Rapide. They improved the engine and cycle parts to a point where, after starting in mid-1947, it had become by the end of the year a very successful hill climbing and road racing machine. For instance, on 11 October 1947, George raced the machine at Dunholme Lodge in the Hutchinson 100, where he came second, being only beaten by the AJS work's Porcupine. After the race was over he popped on a silencer and number plates and promptly rode back home to Stevenage. George continued to race the bike for many following seasons. It was the de-facto factory works racer and was immortalised by the name '*Gunga Din*', so named by *Motor Cycling* writer and tester George Markham after he had been given a test ride only a few days after the Hutchinson 100, when allegedly he found the machine far too fast for his capabilities. The phrase from Rudyard Kipling's poem of that name came supposedly into his mind: 'You are a better man that I am, Gunga Din'. Records show, however, that perhaps his modesty played its part as he had bravely ridden it over a weekend. His weekend ride included a run from Stevenage to Yorkshire via Huddersfield and Bradford, riding through countryside, main roads and town centres, and returning in wet autumn weather while still touching 110 mph in places. This performance proved he certainly gave the machine his best. If nothing else, the performance of the two Georges had proved, while being exceptionally fast, the reliability and flexibility of *Gunga Din* had not been adversely affected by the modifications done to the machine.

When PCV arrived back from a visit to the USA he was enthusiastic about the project and felt this heralded a new sports model (initially he called it the 'Vincent Sports Rapide'). He presented to the board a plan to produce the machine alongside the standard Rapide. His proposal met with opposition by the board in the person of F. E. Walker, the managing director. This opposition was not an unexpected difficulty to PCV, since PCV's father, to curb what he felt were the possible excesses of his inventive son, had installed Mr Walker pre-war at the creation of the company. However, by 1947 Mr Walker was an old man and it was quite easy for the two Phils and George to go ahead and create a couple of the new Sports Rapides without his knowledge.

Above: A view of the factory with Series 'B' Rapide engines in work. The far engine is partly assembled, the rest await the flywheels and barrels etc. from the bench in the background. Clearly this is pure batch production. (Picture courtesy of the Vincent HRD Owners Club)

Right: The first Black Shadow. This is an untouched picture of the prototype Series 'B' Black Shadow. Note the saucepan speedometer housing, which indicates its early nature, but there are many other indications as well. (Photo supplied by Mortons Media Archive)

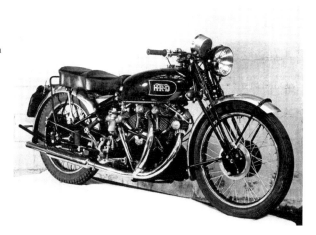

The Selling Points

Long before the term USP (Unique Selling Point) was coined, PCV, with one eye as ever on what would help sell his machines, made three decisions, which to some engineers would have been of minor importance, but he knew would become the selling points that would help make the Black Shadow one of the most iconic machines of the motor age. While history records PCV as responsible for these three salient points, the fact is fate also had a hand in the creation of the legend. Marcus Bowden, who was a ship's engineer and a friend of PCV, told the following story, quoted in his own words:

> Until he had his first stroke, I visited PCV on numerous occasions. My visits came when at the end of each voyage; I left the passenger-banana boats (SS Golfito or SS Camito) at Southampton. Then I would hire a car and detour via Mr Vincent's home with the usual offerings of a 40 oz bottle of whisky and a stem of bananas. He always took the full bottle of whisky, but only cut off a few hands of bananas! Many discussions ensued, mostly about his new engine, but he was also happy to discuss adaptations to it for marine use (he had a wonderful way of selling you his product to match your requirements). He also reminisced occasionally about the works; he said he wouldn't have survived so long if hadn't been for the Black Shadow. He said they had such a stockpile of crankcases that had all been machined ready to build, but when being tested whilst submerged in water with blanks fitted to all apertures, the application of compressed air often revealed porous cases. This underwater testing only came about when they weighed up the wasted man-hours that were involved if they built a complete bike only to find after road testing that it oozed oil through the castings. So, typical of a manufacturer with a poor product, PCV devised a method to seal the cases by submerging them into a vat of shellac, pulling a vacuum, by extracting the air and then on releasing the vacuum, the shellac had as expected been sucked into the cases. Following this they were cleaned off and coated with yellow chromate and stove enamelled black (this gave a nice shiny overcoat but was reputedly poor at dispersing heat).

So, it would seem circumstances helped nudge one of the major selling points of the Black Shadow into reality. Although nowadays it would not seem an unusual decision to paint the engine black, this action should be viewed in the context of the late forties. Cast-iron cylinders and heads had for decades been painted black, but this was for reasons of rust prevention and heat transference. Generally, however, the tradition of gearboxes, crankcases, and where possible also primary chain cases, being polished to a high shine was sacrosanct and embedded deep in the psyche of motorcycling. Although fate and poor castings did have a hand in forcing the situation, reverting to the black paint on the crankcases was still a courageous decision.

With the engine complete in its matching covers, all now in a sombre black, the next act was for PCV to name the machine something a little more resounding than the Vincent Sports Rapide.[6] Perhaps with a nod to the Rolls Royce Silver Shadow, the name Black Shadow was selected, creating the second major selling point.

The last major selling point came from a simple observation that the standard 3-inch speedometer was not capable of displaying the expected top speed of the machine. From the requirements of a dial that displayed well in excess of 120 mph grew the idea for a large 5-inch instrument. This was supplied by Smiths and supposedly without too much effort, since the internal mechanisms were the same as the smaller ones and large dials were common in motorcars. The initial Smiths rendition, believed to be from a Jaguar, was too ugly for PCV, whereupon he promptly placed the works inside a black-painted saucepan, which to this day can be seen on the prototype Black Shadow. This had the desired effect of forcing the supplier into collaborating in designing a more acceptable shape. The final design was a dial reaching 150 mph with the almost unobtainable goal of all other current

Right: A rear view of the prototype Black Shadow showing the face view of the first 5-inch speedometer. The condition of the rear tyre is perhaps a bit too authentic for today's restorers. (Photo supplied by Mortons Media Archive)

Below: The final 5-inch speedometer; this is a newly refurbished unit. At the bottom left of the picture a replica 'lighthouse' dipswitch can be seen. The controls and positions reflect the rider's choice with twin pull twist grip, lightened steering damper knob etc. The round object on the far offside of the top link is a cast VOC badge. (Photo courtesy of BSK Speedworks)

motorcycles – the 'ton' or 100 mph being almost contemptuously reduced to a mere mark without an engraved number.

The Engine and Frame Number

Having detailed the three obvious items that determine a Black Shadow from a Rapide, let us now delve into the specifications of the Shadow and see how it differs in detail.

A Vincent engine number is built up as follows: F (four stroke) 10 (1,000 cc) A (Aluminium) B (Bicycle) / 1B (Black Shadow) or 1A (White Shadow) followed by the number that comprised four digits until around the end of 1952, after which it comprised five digits.

The frame number consists of R (Series 'B') RC (Series 'C') followed by a number, which started out at 2,000 higher than the engine number, but reduced over time to just 1,900. Again this comprised four digits until mid-1951 and then five. Finally, the number had a suffix letter, which was B for Black Shadow, and both the headstock and the left-hand rear frame lug were stamped with this same number. It's worth remembering that the DVLA is reported as regarding only the one on the headstock as the correct designation.

Thus, the marks that add so much to the value of a Black Shadow in the auction houses of the world (all other things being equal) are a 1B on the engine and a B on the frame.

Finally, a warning: the identification of a machine and confirming its authenticity is not an exact science. There are exceptions to the rule and it is advisable to consult the VOC Machine Registrar for authentication and further information.

Engine

A larger 1⅛-inch carburettor was specified; this meant originally the front carburettor had difficulty reaching to the right-hand float bowl, but Amals then produced a specially made left-hand version, which rectified this. The carburettor adaptors were changed for strength from alloy to bronze as the walls of the alloy ones became too thin once opened out. The internals of the bronze adaptors were blended into a smooth

View of an original reconditioned front carburettor; the bronze inlet adaptor can be clearly seen. (Photo courtesy of BSK Speedworks)

contour to match and the ports were matched and polished. The pistons were changed to give an initial uplift of the compression ratio to 7.3:1, which was about as high as the petrol of the time could support.

The engines components were selectively picked, assembled, and tested, and although the cams were still noted as Mark 1s and were nominally the same as the Rapide, in practice the policy was that those with a longer timing were selected for the Black Shadow. The con rods and valve rockers were polished, as were the combustion chambers. Triple valve springs were initially used, but were soon dropped back to two. This selective assembly and alterations were reputed to have boosted power by 10 bhp to 55 bhp.

Transmission

The gearbox first (bottom) gear ratio was altered to 7.25 from the Rapide's 9:1. It was possibly supposed that no-one expected this beast to pull a double adult sidecar. The clutch and cam plate were drilled, making them lighter to improve gear change speed. The original gear change lever, with its quickly wearing linkage, had been replaced by many Series 'B' Rapide owners with a conventional lever direct to the box shaft. In an example of customer initiated design modification, the factory soon responded with its own direct lever, with a multi-positioned pedal and rubber. This modification was incorporated in time to cover most, but not all, of the Black Shadow production.

Frame and Suspension

Frame, steering and suspension were generally unaltered from the Rapide. The Black Shadow production continued initially to use the same Brampton Forks.

Wheels and Brakes

Wheels were unaltered, but by the time of the introduction of the Black Shadow the drums were now of cast iron rather than steel. They were improved for the Black Shadow by adding a set of ribs to the front pair and the same less one rib to allow for

The front ribbed brake drums with aluminium water shields. (Photo by Tim Kingham)

The hubs of a Black Shadow awaiting rebuild into new rims. On the left is the rear ten-hole hub and on the right is the front five-hole hub. One of the original fibre nuts (nowadays replaced with 'nylock' nuts) and the top of one of the original eccentric headed bolts are also visible. The bolts are temporarily locating the spoke flanges in place for wheel building; later they will secure the hubs in position. (Photo courtesy of BSK Speedworks)

sprocket bolts on the rear pair. These ribs added strength as well as improving the heat dissipation. The rear drums also differed in that they were secured by ten bolt holes to the hub, rather than the five used on the front and all drums on the Rapide. The brake lining material was up-rated.

Electrics

The electrics were changed, as regrettably the more productive 3.5-inch dynamo standard was dropped by the industry and replaced by a 3 inch. Those changes were also soon incorporated into the Rapide as well. The headlight fitted was the Miller 6-and a-half-inch type. The standard magneto remained as a KVF type, but it was specified as 'Laboratory Tested'. However, this designation was dropped towards the end of 1950.

Finish

In terms of finish, apart from the black engine and the 5-inch speedometer, there was little to distinguish the rest of the Black Shadow from the Rapide. The engine finish was a black-painted surface applied to the crankcases, covers, heads and barrels, but probably not to the inspection caps. The paint was stove enamel, oven baked on for a couple of hours. More importantly, the process was preceded by an aluminium treatment called polymerisation, which as far as can be ascertained is now obsolete, but was a form of chemical immersion similar to anodising without electrical current being applied. The crankcases (all sand cast) for Series 'B' and 'C' were prepared rather differently from the Rapide cases before painting. In particular it is believed that for Black Shadows, in most cases, the raised portion for the number stamping was ground off.

Conclusion

The above is hardly a long list and there are surprisingly few physical differences that define a Black Shadow, but even those differences could have been eroded by the original customer, as a detailed read of the individual build sheets will reveal. Worrying about such distinctions were, however, in the future, nothing could lessen its impact on the world on the day of the 24 February 1948, when its creation was released to a motorcycle world. For a world still in shock over the performance of the Rapide, to then hear the announcement that a sports version was now available was an absolute bombshell to a country that was, back then, used to real bombshells.

The announced performance was, to most readers, an unbelievable 90 mph in less than fifteen seconds, with a top speed of 128 mph, and came with a price tag of £381.

Chapter Four

Production, Improvements, and Performance

The World in 1948

At this point we should pause to examine the world the Black Shadow was to inhabit, and the UK in particular. The average yearly wage was under £500 and most raw materials were only supplied to companies who were exporting the lion's share of their production. Food and clothes rationing was still in place and in many ways rationing was stricter than during the recent conflict. Bread, for instance, went on ration in 1946, the National Service Act as instituted in 1939 was still in place, and many men were still in the armed services. To buy an average house a sum of £1,750 would have been needed.

It's difficult to really get a feel for what it was like on the roads of Britain in 1948. Statistics are not much help as they state there were around a million cars on the roads. It would be ten more years before the first motorway would be built and there were precious few dual carriageways. Most of the vehicles were pre-war and had passed their tenth birthday. The Jaguar XK120 was reputedly a 120-mph car, which started production about the same time as the Black Shadow and also took a year or so to reach full production, so the Jaguar's performance could hardly be called typical. When and if a new family car could be obtained and run, like the Hillman Minx, the owner would find its maximum speed would be in the region of 70 mph, taking nearly forty seconds to reach 60 mph.

Motorcycles faired a little better in performance terms; 100 mph plus seemed to be almost unreachable even for a solo. Anything that was powered by the big vee-twin JAP like the SS100 Brough Superior might nudge 110 mph in the pre-war period, but they were very rare machines. In total, perhaps 400 were produced and post-war they were no longer made. There was also the Vincent's Series 'A' twin, but less than eighty of those were made. Autocycles, small motorcycles and motorcycles with sidecars abounded.

It doesn't take much imagination to think what it would have been like travelling in a car, behind a slower vehicle for mile after mile along twisting roads. With a fast motorcycle, however, once a solo had passed the obstruction, the empty roads would become a sheer delight, with the few speed limits only within towns. Most towns and villages had a petrol station and garage, which brings to mind the biggest hurdle that would have spoiled a journey: petrol was still 'pool'. For the general public, the only petrol available had an octane rating of around seventy and was unobtainable until June 1948, when rationing was reintroduced. Petrol for commercial use was stained red and checks were often made. Rationing of petrol continued until May 1950.

A view showing the sort of transportation with which the Vincent shared the uncluttered roads in 1948. However, representative as it is, it should be said that the bike is a 1950 Black Shadow and, judging by the Bantam spats on the fork spring covers, the racing brake plates and the modified front number plate position, the actual picture date could be a couple of years later. (Image supplied by Stilltime Collection www. stilltimecollection.co.uk)

The factory records show the first Black Shadow was not completed until April 1948 and the majority of the Black Shadow output went straight to export. The lucky recipients were situated mostly in Argentina, America, Australia, and Cuba.

World Records

Not long after the launch, an order was received from John Edgar in the United States for a Black Shadow to attempt the American land speed record. The factory duly obliged and supplied an up-rated Black Shadow with high lift cams, 85-ton Vibrac rods, larger carburettors, and compression ratios tailored for methanol fuel. Naturally, George Brown had to try it out on a local aerodrome runway, where he achieved 145 mph before having to shut down before he ran out of space. Shipped to the USA, it sailed into the history as the 'bathing suit bike' when Rollie Free, who was the actual rider, took the record at 150.3 mph. It is of note that not only was history made, a new model had also evolved; in the same way that the Rapide had evolved into the Black Shadow, the Black Shadow had now evolved into what the factory was pleased to call in the publicity that followed the world record 'The Black Lightning Racing Rapide'. Undoubtedly, the crankcase did bear the 1B designation and it certainly was supplied

A replica of the original poster that announced the record. The text shows that actual model name of the machine was, at the time, still developing. (Photo Tim Kingham)

as a Black Shadow with special customer requested modifications, but it has often been construed as one of the few, if not the only, Series 'B' Black Lightning. Some additional confusion may also arise, since it is often thought the bathing suit bike had the later Girdraulic forks, but in fact they were Brampton forks, which had been wrapped in tape by Rollie to improve streamlining. To also add to the confusion, later in 1950 Rollie Free did in fact order a Black Lightning for his own use in record attempts.

The Series 'C'

The new models were launched under the generic name 'Series 'C', when they were announced at the 1948 autumn Motorcycle Show. Care should be exercised with the word launched, as it should not be viewed in the mindset of the twenty-first century. While at the show a new model was shown and announced, a complete new model did not really supersede the old one. There was no new production line to be started. Wholesale retooling did not occur. As explained, changes in specification continued before and after that date, but the announcement of the Series 'C' does give a convenient point to note the changes that had been made to the original Series 'B' specifications.

The most notable change visible at the show was the introduction of the Girdraulic fork. The name was formed from the words Girder & Hydraulic.[7] The use of

Girdraulic forks shown here in loosely assembled form without lower spring boxes, handlebar clamps and only one set of spindle nuts attached. In order to fit the bottom of the standard spring box onto the lower fork ear, the springs inside the telescopic spring box needed to be compressed; this is a job that needs to be carried out with the forks on the bike and a great deal of ingenuity and forethought. (Photo courtesy of BSK Speedworks)

aluminium forgings was nothing short of revolutionary. It was common practice for scutineers at race meetings to seize the handlebars of contemporary telescopic forked machines while holding the front wheel between their knees, then to twist and turn the assembly to ensure the flexure was not excessive. On encountering a Girdraulic forked Vincent, however, they were in danger of pulling a muscle since nothing would move. An additional feature was the rake of the Girdraulic fork could simply be adjusted for sidecar use. A Black Shadow was tested on 11 August 1949 by the *Motor Cycle*. The recorded speed was 110 mph in third and with a flair for showmanship that even eclipses PCV's efforts in that regard, instead of quoting a maximum speed in top gear, they reported that immortal phrase 'maximum speed not obtained'. In actual fact, they had uttered the same phrase two years before, when they tested the Series 'B' Rapide. However, on this latest occasion the time for the quarter mile was a second quicker and the terminal speed at 96 mph was 10 mph faster.

The Changes

In practice, and true to form, the changes came in gradually. Supplies of the new fork were sporadic and bikes continued to be produced with Brampton forks as well as Girdraulics. When Girdraulics were available, they were fitted on a first-come first-served basis. Once the Series 'C' was announced, it must have proved difficult to move the stocks of those bikes fitted with Bramptons. This is reflected in part by the price list in the March 1949 editions of *The Motorcycle,* where prices were quoted as £400 1s 0d for the 'C' Black Shadow and £381 0s 0d for the 'B' Black Shadow. Sometime in 1950 supplies were adequate and from then on Brampton's were rarely ever fitted.

The bottom gear ratio for the Black Shadow reverted to the Rapide 9:1 – whether by request of users or cost cutting is not clear. For all models the clutch linings were changed to Duron with a revised seal added. Both of these changes were aimed at reducing the effects of and the ingress of oil, which could easily affect the clutch efficiency. Spirited riding early on had allowed the bottom of the clutch cover to hit the road, therefore a chamfer at the bottom was introduced to obtain more clearance.

Now that the buying public had decided rear springing was acceptable, the mainstream motorcycle industry was slowly crystallising suspension design around swinging arms with twin shock absorbers at the rear and improved telescopic forks at the front. One factor that had prompted the change was the improvement of hydraulics during the war, on aeroplane undercarriages and gun recoil mechanisms. By the 1950s this technology had percolated down to the motor industry. PCV had recognised that fact and, although he maintained his objections to those telescopic fork designs, he was happy to employ hydraulics in conjunction with the rigidity of his existing Girdraulic fork and RFM. He decided to have new Vincent hydraulic dampers to fit both ends of the machine. There was, unfortunately, nothing commercially available off the shelf, so these were designed for Vincent by an outside body, after which their components were probably mostly manufactured in-house. The hydraulic dampers worked very well when new.

Notable among obvious changes was the replacement of the HRD name with that of the Vincent name on the crankcase and petrol tank. Not only was this due to the

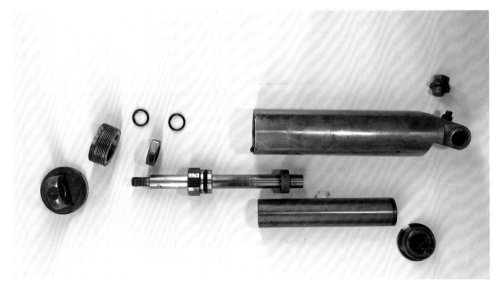

The standard damper components. The rod is screwed into the top 'eye' and locked with a small pin. The periphery of the top eye locates the tubular shroud (not shown). (Photo by Tim Kingham)

American market, then as now mesmerised with HD Harley Davidson and confusing that with HRD, but also it was almost twenty-five years since HRD had scored that victory in the 1925 TT and memories were growing dim. Again, this was not an immediate changeover and in the end stocks of castings with HRD on them sometimes had all legends removed to assist sales.

The original timing cover with the raised oil ways had earlier been replaced with a smoother design and it now incorporated a small 'VINCENT' cartouche in the centre rather than the 'HRD'. The UFM underwent a major change in 1951 when the head lug at the front of the UFM was made to slot inside a revised cylinder head bracket rather than the previous design, where the lug straddled a solid bracket.

A twin plate damper at the bottom of the steering head replaced the single plate damper. To improve brake action, a stop pin was added to the brake beam plate on the front in conjunction with a return spring and new cable. The modification was noted and dimensioned in *Vincent Motor Cycles* so owners could retrofit it to earlier machines.

The prop stands were increased in length to suit the altered suspension. As with the series 'B', alternative touring equipment was available.

Competition

Probably at the behest of the major manufacturers, worried about their various racers and road bikes being decimated by the Stevenage twins, the Racing Authorities imposed capacity limits on many headline races. In spite of this there were still quite a few races at home and abroad in which the bikes were eligible, and during the forties and fifties many races were won by Vincent big twins. It is difficult at this distance in time to distinguish those won by Rapides, 'Shadowised' Rapides, Black Shadows, 'lightningised' Black Shadows, or a pure Black Lightning, or many of the other 'mongrel' racers that abounded at that time. Often the results said just '998 Vincent', and when a Black Shadow was quoted as the winner, it could be difficult to know whether it really was one or not.

There were, however, important events and competitions where we can be fairly confident as to the exact Vincent model being used. Three of the best examples are detailed below:

The Clubman's TT

In 1948 the Clubman's TT was run for production bikes – in effect it was a production TT. This was really before the Black Shadow was eligible as a production bike, so it was the Rapides that performed in the race. John Daniels came first and Phil Heath came second, with George Brown coming sixth when he had to push home the length of the Glencutry Road after running out of petrol. George had also set the fastest lap. It would seem this great performance by the Vincent twins was as unexpected as it was comprehensive. The British Motorcycle Industry complacent as ever, was caught on the hop. They had not expected what they had called before the race as, the 'cumbersome' machines from Stevenage, to achieve that result. If the win was not enough to panic the big fish of the British Motorcycle Industry, a prototype Black Shadow being ridden on the island in the same TT week by a member of the *Motorcycling* magazine staff revealed a top speed of 122 mph! Accordingly, steps were taken to pull the teeth of the Stevenage upstart. This was accomplished for the following year, by separating the classes by capacity, reducing the laps to three and removing refuelling. It was clear that a standard Vincent Black Shadow was not going to easily run for 113 miles on its 3-gallon or so standard tank. So the next year, the first Vincent home ridden by Dennis Lashmar averaged just over 76 mph, while George's fastest lap time the previous year had been 82.6 mph.

In 1950 the refuelling was once again allowed, but riders with previous island experience were banned, as was the warm up period, so it was goodbye to the recommendation for the equivalent of 15 miles of warm up before using the Black Shadow's full potential. As a final restriction, starting was by kick-start, which probably resulted in the employment of many prayers being offered to the god of easy kick-starts.

The fastest man in practice was Alex Philips on an upgraded 1947 Rapide. J. Alexander Edwards, however, had a new Black Shadow from the factory, and although he led the race in the early stages, it was Philips who won, with Edwards second. For the winner, the average lap speed was still slower than 1948, but in mitigation it should be noted the weather was far from ideal. The results did show a modified and updated Rapide was on the same terms as a new Black Shadow – a point many then current Rapide owners noted with glee. After that the industry seemed to have decided the Clubman's TT was too much of a one horse race and another large capacity production bike race series in the Isle of Man had to wait until 1974.

The 1950 Clubman's TT winner, Alex Philips, in Parliament Square, Ramsey. His Vincent was a 1948 Rapide 'modernised' and carefully assembled with Girdralics and an engine updated to Black Shadow specification. The bike was later sold to Lt Colonel Churchill of the Second World War commando fame, also known as the British war hero 'Mad Jack' Churchill. (Photo supplied by Mortons Media Archive)

Montlhèry

In 1952 it was decided to go to Montlhèry in France, which was a banked concrete bowl circuit, to try to achieve 100 mph for twenty-four hours on a Black Shadow. While it is known the attempt failed, the failure has often been blamed on tyres not being able to withstand the punishment, and it was probably in the company's interest to foster that story. The details of the actual attempt are somewhat clouded and several accounts have been given.[8] What seems certain is that it arose because a batch of three or four other bikes described as 'Black Lightnings', perhaps including *Gunga Din*, were also taken to the track at the same time as two or three 'Montlhèry' Black Shadows.[9] It was the 'Lightnings', who in attempting some of the short duration records on a very hot day, lost huge strips of their rear tyres at 130 to 140 mph. Having researched a number of accounts, it is thought the Black Shadow record events unfolded as follows: the first Black Shadow twenty hour attempt started well enough, as it circulated happily in

A picture of the pits during the Montlhèry record breaking attempt. It is apparent that the Black Shadows were not quite standard, apart from the obvious big tank and lack of front brake there were other detailed modifications. Notable among these were: only one rear brake drum was fitted, the carburettors were TT and 1/16th larger than standard, and the engines were extensively blueprinted and ran on open lightning pipes. However, it is fair to claim that they were in essence Black Shadows. (Photo supplied by Mortons Media Archive)

the extreme heat, hitting 130 mph on the straights, but just before the six hour record could fall, the standard big end failed. It was said by PCV that Vic Willougby, the third rider, had pushed the bike too hard, which resulted in him being taken off the team. When the second attempt started, the aim of a more reasonable, at a perhaps more supervised pace, was maintained of just over 102 mph plus, including tyre, rider, and fuel stops, until when just over ten hours had elapsed, the second machine also seized its big end. By pushing the bike round to the start they managed to gain the eleven hour record, having previously also captured some of the other records. Nevertheless, considering the original avowed target of the twenty-four hour record was not achieved, and while recognising the fact that they obtained some good publicity about those records they did manage to break, it must be considered a failed attempt. It was said, had the racing caged big end been fitted, the attempt would have been a success. Ted Davis had originally fitted a caged big end assembly, but said PCV had insisted on it being replaced with a standard one. PCV's version of events was that he had calculated the maximum revs to be sustained while the target speed was maintained, and because of that restriction he was happy to employ the crowded standard big end since he felt it was important to demonstrate the reliability of what was available as standard. Unfortunately, he had not expected the grade and type of oil insisted on by the sponsoring oil company to be so woefully inadequate when used in the exceptional heat encountered in that early spring at the track. This lack of correct lubrication was confirmed when on stripping the engine after the event, there was disastrous wear on the cams and followers. Whatever the sequence of events and wherever the blame should have fallen, it was a bitter disappointment that was skilfully camouflaged by some good publicity.

Tony Rose

A private detective, Tony Rose, bought a new Black Shadow. At the 1951 Earls Court motor show, he asked PCV what sort of mileage he thought a Black Shadow should be able to cover without a major rebuild. PCV replied 100,000 miles, adding a proviso that he should not exceed 5,000 rpm. Tony was the man to prove that estimation as he was in a job that entailed high mileage. So, with just 8,900 miles on the clock already, with the support of the VOC and sponsorship from Filtrate Oil, he continued to ride it solo and with a sidecar. In particular, he was always careful to allow the engine to warm up before using its full performance, yet he was not taking it easy as, during the test, he had seen 110 mph solo and 90 mph with a sidecar, averaging 200 miles a day. A large proportion of his travelling was during the night, so his biggest criticism was the performance of the standard lights. With that daily average he took only one year to complete the 100,000 miles without a major rebuild.

One should not, however, gain the impression that there was no maintenance involved, as he reputedly used fifty-five rear tyres, twenty-five rear chains, three exhaust systems, twenty sets of plugs, six sets of brake linings, and three sidecars. Tony also wore out three seats, as it was not unusual back then for a Vincent to stand outside in all weathers, especially as the bike was in almost constant use.[10]

To round off the amazing exercise, it so happened the target mileage was reached in Scotland in January in a blizzard. As fate would have it, the speedometer cable broke just as the last hundred or so miles were racked up, which meant Tony was missing

Tony Rose and Jim Regan. The bike is shown in sidecar trim, as it was for over three quarters of the test. When PCV had said the Black Shadow would do 100,000 miles without major repairs, he was thinking it was as a solo! (Photo supplied by Mortons Media Archive)

that final confirmation. Undaunted, he repaired the cable and rode back to Stevenage for the strip down and inspection, so then the speedometer would read correctly over 100,000 miles travelled. Thus, PCV's estimate of 100,000 miles was proven correct, in that it had not been necessary to disturb the engine.

Chapter Five

The Next Model

The Series 'D'

It became clear by 1954 that the design of the Vincent was becoming outdated. It was still, in terms of potential performance, head and shoulders above anything the rest of the motorcycle industry could make, and would continue to be so for the next ten years, but the little factory in Stevenage had little to challenge the advertising budgets of the volume manufacturers. The other annoyance was that the capacity limits imposed on racing in all the premier events – in particular the TT – ensured the eyes of a fickle public looking for speed were held firmly elsewhere. Another factor by then was most contemporary machines had belatedly caught up and settled into a fully sprung, dual-seated design. Now it was the Vincent that was considered by some to look outdated.

   Part of this stagnation of design was due to the resources that had been absorbed by a project that involved producing a version of the twin engine called the Picador. This engine was developed to power an early unmanned drone for the Air Ministry, which was planned for use in gunnery target practice. This would have been the salvation of the motorcycle production, as the increased demand for the engines thus generated would have made the continued production of motorcycles an economic certainty. Sadly this was not to be. The engine was fitted into a number of test aircraft and, although the engine performed well, the remote radio controls did not. After Vincents had spent a lot of time in engine development work, the Air Ministry dropped the project. This was a repeat of the situation with a marine engine project at the end of the war and emphasised how hard it was for a small factory to rely on peacetime government projects to provide a steady income. It was now felt something radical must be done in time for the autumn 1954 motorcycle show, but PCV's scope for development was severely limited by the parlous state of the company's finances and perhaps by the fact that Phil Irving was no longer available to discuss improvements with, since he had left the company some time before. So PCV turned for assistance to a source that knew the existing design well – he asked the Vincent HRD Owners Club (VOC) by way of a survey in its monthly journal *MPH* what they would like to see in a new Vincent. When the results were announced from the 137 responses, the majority of the requirements were a larger petrol tank, more electrical power, a fully sprung headlight, shorter handlebars, a cush drive in the rear hub, an enclosed final drive chain, and nearly all wanted a fully sprung seat. Amazingly, considering the date, many called for disc brakes, or at least 'Alfin' drums. Tellingly in the engine department, most were satisfied with the status quo, except some wanted coil ignition and a fewer oil leaks.

The New Model Revealed

When the Series 'D' was announced in the autumn of 1954 it was another PCV design stunner. The completely enclosed bikes were like nothing ever seen before. They were so futuristic that in the following year they were used as the Thought Polices' motorcycles in the film adaptation of the George Orwell novel *1984*. The entire motorcycle (there were two basic models) was clothed in a set of enclosures that provided protection from the elements and was proven to be stable in crosswinds. It is perhaps a coincidence, but it was actually around 1984 before another manufacturer would produce a motorcycle with such performance and protection that was acceptable to the general public. The plan of introduction of the Series 'D' was that the Black Knight would replace the Rapide and the Black Prince would replace the Black Shadow. However, the proposed enclosures were in fibreglass – a process that, at that time, was the cutting edge of industrial production technology, and the suppliers were a long time in obtaining a satisfactory quality for use by Vincents. In fact, when the models were to be unveiled for the 1954 show at Olympia, the enclosures were the product of a lot of last minute preparation work because of the poor quality of the finish; in fact, the quality was so bad PCV had to change to a new supplier, which resulted in months of delay. Faced with such a hiatus, the gap was plugged in desperation by the introduction of a new Black Shadow and Rapide in 'open' 'D' format. To some, they looked a little ungainly;

The Series 'D' at Olympia. Not only did it take a lot of work to get the glass fibre bodywork to an acceptable appearance, the lorry taking the machines to the exhibition crashed and they had to do much of the work again! (Image supplied by Stilltime Collection www.stilltimecollection.co.uk)

An open Series 'D' created from the necessity of filling a production gap until the enclosure quality was acceptable. Not in all honesty a beautiful machine. (Photo by Pamela Horrell)

they stood higher in the seat, the steering damper assembly jutted out because it was intended to be within enclosures, gone was the front aluminium cowling and instead a steel cover enclosed the distributor, and a Lucas ignition coil was attached to the crankcase over the primary drive cover.

The introduction of die-cast crankcases a little earlier meant that with the new models the black paint finish could be removed from the crankcases, as it followed that under enclosures its absence would not be noticed. Once the open models were hurriedly introduced, however, the black finish was maintained on the covers to partially retain the tradition – a decision that helpfully also saved on polishing costs. One result of this change meant that while the different engine specifications between the two models were maintained, both the Rapide and Black Shadow engines now had the same external appearance; in fact, they looked so alike, a 'Black Shadow' script was added to the tank of the open Series 'D' Black Shadow to emphasise the difference. In use, the 'D' Black Shadow, indeed all the 'D' variants, were reported to have better road holding, but in general it was also felt the sporting aspects of the beast had been obscured. This supposition was made concrete when the enclosed machines (the open 'D's were never tested) were taken to the then new MIRA test track and timed electronically. After some changing of carburettor settings, it would seem that 110 mph from the Prince and slightly less from the Knight was all that could be reliably expected at that time. It is assumed the small changes in design, a drop in quality in machining and fitting, plus the increases in frontal area and weight had all contributed

When viewed in a contemporary setting, the cars, the pumps, the attendant, and the rider and his clothing all emphasise the fact the enclosed Series 'D' was a design far ahead of its time. This is Vic Willoughby during a test of an early Black Knight. (Image supplied by Stilltime Collection www.stilltimecollection.co.uk)

to the fall in performance. For many that was the end of the discussion, because then, perhaps as now, ultimate performance seemed to sell bikes and it mattered not that Vic Willoughby (*The Motorcycle*, Nov. 1954) covered 500 miles up and down the A1 on a winter's day on a Black Knight, averaging 53 mpg.

The Changes in Detail

The changes to both models reflected a number of factors: the VOC questionnaire recommendations, the changes in component availability by suppliers, design improvements and, unfortunately, also an element of cost cutting. Apart from the fairings, the major changes that reflected the Series 'D' were better suspension by use of longer and softer suspension actuated by Armstrong dampers and a sub frame supporting a fully sprung seat. A larger tank with the existing outer pressings was also possible because the UFM oil tank was replaced with a tubular member. The oil tank and toolbox were situated at the sides of the new seat support frame. Carburetion was changed to the then new Amal product, the Monoblock. There was better lighting equipment from Lucas, including a 60-watt dynamo and regulator, and a front brake stoplight switch that illuminated a more effective rear light. At the front was fitted a 7-inch headlamp unit from Morris Minor in a shell similar to that fitted to the Sunbeam shaft drive motorcycle. In the headlamp shell resided a built in speedometer.

Introduced at the same time as the Series 'D', the Monoblock carburettor is often retrofitted to the Series 'C'. The example in this picture has a longer intake bellmouth than standard. The finned component on the dynamo clamp is a more modern rectifier casing. (Photo by Angela Kingham).

One concession was the intended Black Prince and the hastily revamped open Black Shadow speedometer was calibrated to 150 mph, while the touring variants were only 120 mph, but this was little recompense for the loss of the 5-inch instrument, which was not continued. As far as Lucas was concerned, magnetos were a dying application and so ignition was changed to the far cheaper coil ignition, which it was said would improve starting. The front and rear stands were removed to be replaced by a centre stand, actuated with a large lever reminiscent of the pre-war Rudge. This made putting the machine on a stand a far easier task, but in the workshop or on sloping ground it was not as convenient as the previous arrangements. The wheel sizes were reduced to 19-inch front and 18-inch rear, which reflected the option in the previous touring specification. Design changes adjacent to the rear wheel included the removal of one of the rear drums, the Tommy bar wheel spindles, and the rear click adjusters. One obvious change that was partly a cost saver and partly a nod to the modifying owners was that two 'front' heads were employed on the front and rear cylinders, rather than the previous two different castings. The idler boss in the timing case was replaced with a more robust one-piece item. The Series 'D' dropped the timed breather and adopted a modified upper valve guide base and a breather connection on the modified front exhaust valve spring cap. The steel pushrod tubes were replaced by aluminium ones, but due to material changes or perhaps machining errors, some had the habit of leaking oil. It was found the engine ran cooler because of the remote oil tank.

The VOC members' dreams were partially realised in the Series 'D', but there were no improvements to brakes or transmission. No doubt a parked Series 'D' could possibly mark its territory with an oil leak, just like a Series 'C' and, supposedly, if they wanted 3 inches off the handlebars, the new owner could always resort to the hacksaw. There was also no doubt that like the owners survey replies, the Series 'D' specification had little new to offer to those with sporting pretentions.

The End of Production

The last Series 'C' Black Shadow was made sometime in December 1954, which was sold in February 1955. Also around that time, the fully enclosed Series 'D' began to emerge from the factory to join the open Series 'D' Black Shadow and Rapide, which also continued in production. Sadly, the writing was on the wall and towards the end of 1955 the announcement came that production of the Series 'D' motorcycle was to end. It would seem enthusiasts could dream of sophistication and would happily help to compile a specification, while at the same time keeping their existing machines. The general buying public may well have just regarded the enclosed Series 'D' as an expensive glorified scooter, which, in spite of evidence to the contrary, they felt would be unstable in side winds, and they seemed to prefer the ever-cheapening lure of the car, or the uncomfortable stance of the 'ton up boys' machines.

The Inquest

It has long been a winter's occupation in VOC meeting rooms around the country to discuss the reasons for the failure of the Vincent Company. Bad luck played its part with the failure of many projects and the government as a customer, and sales partners like NSU did not always do what had been expected. Mostly, this occurred without any fault directly attributed to the company, but perhaps it basically came down to the hard fact that the Vincent was too good a product for its market. It was and still is a motorcycle that doesn't wear out quickly and whose parts can be easily interchanged. The big twins performance was so far ahead of the big manufacturers machines, hampered as they were by 'just enough' cost limits and maximum profits, that they were happy to crowd Vincent off from the oxygen of publicity. Vincent's advanced design features were not, unfortunately, the sales features that were a 'must have' feature of the mid-fifties market place; as time has told, they predated the general buying public expectations and desires by decades. Finally, it must be said that a significant element in the company's demise was the devaluation of the Black Shadow icon. The loss of those big three selling points, the naked black engine appearance, the 5-inch speedometer, and most importantly the loss of the name Black Shadow, had to have played their part in the end of production.

CHAPTER SIX

Modifications

The How's and Why's of Modification

Before dealing in detail with the continued history of the Black Shadow and its effect in the world after the factory closure, it seems suitable at this point to spend some time looking at the various modifications that have been done to the Vincent over the years, with an emphasis on the Black Shadow.

As mentioned earlier, there were few sophisticated manufacturing processes involved in the majority of Vincent components and no lack of enthusiasm on the side of the owners. After the Vincent Owners Club was formed at the end of 1948, club nights and rallies were soon in session up and down the UK and overseas, full of discussions on the latest modifications or alterations. Printed information on modifications to the Vincent was also not difficult to obtain. Apart from the club's magazine, the aptly named *MPH*, and just as production was ending at Stevenage, a new book was published, titled *Vincent Motor Cycles*, affectionately known to enthusiasts as 'Richardson'. The author was Paul Richardson, who had been the service manager of Vincent HRD until 1951. This book was compiled from a lot of factory data and his personal background experience. It was intended to cover all the general maintenance tasks on the bikes, but it also enumerated a number of modifications and upgrades, which were possible, especially those for racing and the upgrading of Rapides to Black Shadow specification.

Modifications seemed to flow as soon as the bikes were on the market. There were many reasons for this; obviously some were for the comfort of the touring or commuter rider, which included different handlebars, handlebar fairings, incorporation of panniers etc. For the majority of Black Shadow owners, the main influence came from the racetrack. A well-known adage is that 'Racing improves the breed' and the racing modifications were soon percolating down the models and the interchangeability of parts aided this. When looking at any old program of a club meeting of the sixties and especially the regular meetings organised and held by the Motor Cycling Club (MCC) at Silverstone, or indeed the VOC itself at Cadwell, it is evident the grids are full of Vincents being raced.

Examination of the accompanying pictures will show not only the external modifications that were made, but also how difficult it is, especially at a distance, to differentiate the two road models and their hybrids. Racing then was an environment of hard competition and not like a sedate classic circuit parade during the lunch break at a modern meeting. Today that stately progressing immaculate Black Shadow being navigated to its place at the club concours by the careful octogenarian quite possibly once battled three abreast into the Cadwell hairpin with a hard pressed engine and

MCC High Speed Trials at Silverstone in July 1960. No. 59 is C. P. Robinson on an enclosed 'D' with a streamliner fairing, No. 79 is C. Camhi and No. 64 is J. Renwick (later to become a renowned sprinter) both on what appear to be Rapides, but both sporting 5-inch speedometers. (Photo by Geoff Preece)

MCC High Speed Trials at Silverstone in June 1962. This is W. M. Pape on what appears to be a Shadow, and some 'racing' modifications are visible; it is sporting a Gold Star silencer and turned down 'ace' type handlebars, the front cowl has been removed, but it is still sporting crash bars. (Photo by Geoff Preece)

MCC High Speed Trials at Silverstone in June 1964. G. W. Clulee on a Black Shadow; note the breather pipe on the track (catch tanks are required nowadays) and the full ace handlebars. The tank and castings sport the HRD badge while the bike has Girdraulic forks. (Photo by Geoff Preece)

VOC Race Day at Cadwell Park in August 1966. No. 44 J. Kinley and No. 41 Malcolm Attrill on *The Fast Lady* sliding round Cadwell hairpin on the old club circuit. As expected both Girdraulic are on sidecar settings with smaller wheels and sidecar tyres. Another Gold Star silencer is fitted on one bike and the other silencer looks 'doctored', both sport auxiliary revcounters driven off the magneto timing side. (Photo by Geoff Preece)

MCC High Speed Trials at Silverstone in July 1968. M. L. Spreadbury was one of the renowned competitors of the Vincent racing scene. This was a very competitive Black Shadow sporting a Gold Star silencer and modified carburettors, with alloy rims and racing brake plates on its Brampton forks, which were preferred by many for circuit racing over Girdraulics. (Photo by Geoff Preece)

VOC Race Day at Cadwell Park in August 1969. The bikes are ready for the unlimited scratch race and are waiting for a full grid. The Black Shadows of No. 36 Alan Johnson and No. 47 Ray Atkinson sandwich the No. 39 Vincent engine special of Robin Hawkins. No. 36 is fitted with full racing brake plates while No. 47 has standard steel ones. The engines of No. 36 and No. 39 have modified coil ignition systems partially visible on the timing cover. The VOC Race Days continued into the mid-nineties. (Photo by Geoff Preece)

smoking locked wheels. A lot of the competition also took place in the workshop as the owners tried to squeeze that last ounce of performance for the next meeting.

This tendency by owners to modify does not imply the original model was badly designed; it was rather the fact it was designed to last and to be updated. It was well over ten years after the factory closed before another standard motorcycle came near the Black Shadow's performance, let alone emulated its innate character. This gave long exposure to riders, who saw no reason to change their machines for an inferior and slower design – they felt they would rather amend the machine to their needs and to incorporate the technological changes that occurred in the decades that followed. After all, their already superior machine was then worth only a fraction of the value of a new machine on the open market.

Now, of course, the values of the machines have risen and the influence of collectors and investors over the last decade or so are becoming apparent; not only do they drive the out of proportion price difference between the Rapide and the Black Shadow, they have almost an obsession and a need to return every aspect of the machine to its original state. It is essential that we do have good examples of the original machines, especially if they are unrestored, but the desire for wholesale refurbishment, while in some ways understandable, is not matched by the way variations actually occurred in production seventy years ago. It has been argued that as they remove modifications that made the machines more compatible for modern riding, they make it less likely for the machine to be used. It has also been said that in removing them to restore them in a pastiche of a 1950s showroom model, they are in a small way also destroying the patina and history of some seventy years of ownership.

Of course, there were many modifications carried out, and when all is considered some were not an improvement. The modifications mentioned below are those that are significant in the history of the machine, though their mention here does not constitute a recommendation to purchase, install, or emulate them. Many of these modifications have reached general acceptance and are stocked by Vincent Owners Club Spares Company Ltd (Vincent Spares) and other suppliers at the present time.[11]

Basic Engine Modifications

As petrol improved higher compression pistons started to be inserted and ignition points were altered. When five-star petrol was introduced, it would be fair to say the ten and eleven to one ratios then possible really detracted from the overall flexibility and smoothness of the twins; no doubt they were also often employed for that small competition advantage at the next club race meeting. When the standard 'Specialoid' pistons were no more, those looking for a suitable replacement generally went to Omega. Later, Ron Kemp, in conjunction with the Vincent Spares Company, developed a low expansion replacement and 'Kempaloid' became the favourite piston name in the clubroom. Nowadays, with the phasing out of leaded petrol, the tendency is to reduce compression ratios to a more reasonable level.

As piston availability and manufacturing techniques improved, one of the modifications that rose to prominence in the 1990s was to increase the capacity of the engine by enlarging the bore of the engine normally to 90 mm. This resulted in an engine size 572 cc per cylinder, which entailed opening up the crankcase mouth for the increased liner diameter. While it was possible to retain the standard studs,

Many alternative pistons have been fitted to the Vincent. A few examples are (left to right): Specialoid, Hepolite, VOC/Kempaloid, Cosworth, Venolia custom. The last two are 'big bore' 90-mm pistons, the others are the standard size of 84 mm. (Photo by Tim Kingham)

Cartridge-type oil filter on the left (top). The original filter element (lower) on the right was made of felt mounted on a wire frame. (Photo by Tim Kingham)

a better solution was to employ two-piece studs that retained the standard end threads, but had a reduced diameter through the muff to reduce the stud hole size, thus increasing its strength. Whichever way it was achieved, a great advantage of this modification was that when installed it was practically invisible. Modifications to further increase capacity by altering bore and stroke were major engineering tasks for special projects.

While suitable for normal road use, the crowded roller big end was often replaced by a caged one, as per the Black Lightning. Indeed, the invaluable manual *Tuning for Speed* written by Phil Irving had a detailed description on a method of producing a crowded roller big end, utilising modified MSS Velocette cages. Although probably not as good as the original pattern one used in the Black Lightning from the factory, the Alpha bearings big end became the normal replacement – especially after Harpers, the successors to the Vincent company, were no longer themselves on the scene.

A twin start worm for the oil pump was available as it had been developed for the ill-fated Picador target drone project; this was often (and still is) taken up by some racers. It was never used on factory racers, has a shorter life and is a doubtful advantage on the low-pressure oil system used on the Vincent. In fact many reports of filler cap froth and oil spillage into riders' faces when racing may be associated with that adaptation. Another often-seen modification on Vincent engines and specials is the use of high-pressure braded stainless steel oil line. These are completely over the top as the original herringbone hose is more than adequate for the stately flow of oil that circulates in the twin engine.

The original felt and wire assembly oil filter located in the oil chamber at the front of the engine, directly under the magneto position, can be replaced by a modern paper cartridge type filter that has better filtering properties than the original design.

Vibrac rods as used in the Black Lightning were never plentiful and as time passed standard rods seemed to be almost as reliable in all but extreme competition. Nowadays, Carrillo rods are available and tend to be employed.

Heads

Many a Comet single was beheaded as owners fitted a front head to the rear cylinder of the twin. This fashion grew from the fact that increasing the front head inlet port diameter ran a smaller risk of breaking through the wall of the head than it did on the rear. It also gave, theoretically, a better inlet path. This change, as mentioned in the description of the Series 'D', was a point taken up by the factory. The exhaust pipe threads were a source of some problems; the fine thread in the aluminium head and the bronze-finned exhaust pipe nut, combined with difficulties in presenting the exhaust flange squarely on assembly, resulted in an attachment problem that was easily overcome with application of skill, patience, and a little copper grease. Sometimes, with some owners, one or all of those requirements were missing, which resulted in cross threading and ruination of the threads. Normal cures are oversize taps and nuts, brass inserts or welding and re-machining a new thread. A solution, which is not recommended, was the insertion of an alloy tube, some welding, and a push-on exhaust pipe and a clamp.

In the late 1960s, valve guide seals became widely available and adopted. After removal of the third valve spring early in the history of the Black Shadow, the valve springs remained unaltered. Some alternatives were used in competition, notably S&W springs, mainly in the USA and BSA Gold Star springs in the UK. Generally, however, the valves springs and associated items seem to have remained largely as designed. A problem arose with the valve gear as time went on, with the wearing of the rocker tunnels by a loose oscillating rocker bearing. Many early 'cures' were tried, such as longer rocker bearings, oversize bearings in bored out tunnels, and increasing

Above left: A 'not to be recommended' modification. Sometimes used when the exhaust nut thread is stripped in the head. The standard arrangement with nut and thread on the exhaust pipe flange reduces heat feed from the exhaust pipe back into the head. This modification does not. (Photo courtesy of Marcus Bowden)

Above right: Two popular methods of overcoming the problem of excess wear in the rocker tunnel. On the top left the ET100/1 locking oil feed bolt and thin nut, below it the standard ET100 oil feed bolt. The hole in the top of the bearing needs slight enlargement and if the retaining 'nut' that fits inside the bearing prevents full movement of the rocker, the rocker may need to be relieved on its top face. On the right is a longer rocker bearing, which provides more bearing area. (Photo courtesy of Vincent Spares)

the diameter of the rocker cross shaft so it was held in the bearing, which allowed a bushed rocker to oscillate on it. Other unmentionable bodges were thought of – even wedges were inserted into the tunnel – but the solution, or rather the prevention, came with the so-called ET100 locking feed bolts. The bolts work effectively, but if fitted, care must be taken that sufficient clearance exists on the rocker movement.

Timing Gear

There were as standard three cam forms from the factory during the production period. Of these, two were road cams – a Mark one and milder Mark three – and the third, which was a racing cam that had been developed for the Black Lightning and Grey Flash, named the Mark two, was also generally available. Many owners fitted these Mark two cams, which were sufficiently mild for road use, but necessitated a shortening of the top guide. Other cam designs have been employed – Somerton, Megacycle, and some exotic types with wild curved followers – but the main stream of users seem to stay with one of the three Vincent variations. There was a burst of needle roller bearing modifications in the late 1960s for the cams, which in the end did not seem to offer any noticeable advantage. Repairs and alterations to the cams can be made with stellite, if carried out correctly, without holes being formed in the weld. This treatment can also be effective on the flat followers, but the latter is done less often nowadays as replacement followers are plentiful. The main cause of problems in the

Above left: Details of the valve lifter abutment options. At the top is a standard valve lifter abutment and on the bottom the modified abutment with improved garter type oil seal. (Photo courtesy of Vincent Spares)

Above right: A Royal Enfield decompressor fitted in a second plug hole in the head. An advantage is the 'lift' of the two cylinders can be varied to allow the rear cylinder to be selected for kick-starting, a disadvantage is they are short reach 'plugs' in the long reach plug hole. (Photo by Tim Kingham)

cam area was that the cam spindles tend to become loose in the crankcase wall. Here, as in many situations on a Vincent, the various loctite products are of assistance, but it really is an engineering job with replacement of the loose spindles using new special spindles with oversize ends.

The valve lifter operates inside the timing cover by lifting the cam followers off the cam base circle by two levers, which has often come in for criticism. The levers are operated by a cable via adjustable links made from wheel spokes and sometimes the hardened rollers in the ends of the levers will drop into the timing gears. In addition, the mechanism frequently allowed oil to escape via its cable abutment entry point in the timing cover. Now a modified abutment is available, which is of a much-improved design. Some owners, however, prefer to use a Royal Enfield decompressor in a second spark plug hole in the cylinder head.

The large idler originally in bronze was replaced with an aluminium one, which was used successfully for many years. However, by the mid-sixties it became evident that under the influence of time and use, the teeth were partially breaking off, often resulting in filling the lower cavities of the engine with smaller particles of alloy and also contaminated the oil. Slowly, every knowledgeable owner joined the racers in fitting a steel Black Lightning-type idler.

It is the subject of breathers that seems to have created the biggest number of modifications and discussions over the years. As standard, the Series 'B' and 'C' twins had a timed breather, which worked well, although in latter years PCV himself

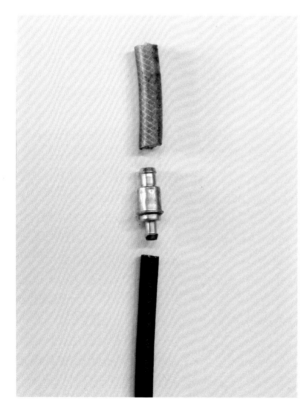

Above left: The three generations of the main idler gear. On the left the original bronze, in the middle the aluminium idler, and on right the steel replacement originally created for the Lightning. (Photo courtesy of Vincent Spares)

Above right: Close up of the 'Elephants Trunk' breather mounted on the magneto drive inspection cover. The six attachment holes are symmetrical so the angle of the outlet pipe is a matter of convenience so long as it remains substantially upright. (Photo by Tim Kingham)

Left: A Positive Crankcase Ventilation valve. The valve contains a one-way ball construction and should be mounted in an upward direction on a short length of pipe before descending on the second pipe to a catch tank, which can be situated in a suitable position at some distance away. With an engine in good condition there is little or no oil at the end of the pipe after use, and once engine has been started and has run for a short time there is very little movement of air. (Photo by Tim Kingham)

suggested widening the opening period. The purpose of any breather system is to give a free path to the air trapped beneath the descending piston, or rather on a vee twin the oscillating volume, without losing any oil mist and, in the case of a timed breather, preventing its return. The early sixties saw a plethora of hoses bedecking the rear of many machines with transparent breather hoses from every orifice, engine, primary and gearbox. Generally perhaps, apart from fashion, this was more than anything else indicative of worn piston rings and valve guides, allowing blow by to increase the crankcase pressure. Soon some common sense prevailed; pipes reduced in size and quantity, many Series 'C' owners took up the Series 'D' method of engine ventilation via the exhaust valve cap, while the elephant's trunk on the magneto cover gained the ascendancy. In turn, those who felt this was an unsightly protrusion – hence the name – were soon fitting compact Positive Crankcase Ventilation valves into their standard breather pipes. These are one-way valves, which work by virtue of a one-way flap or ball. These valves, when positioned correctly, work well, do not drip oil, and should hold the crankcase of a good condition motor at or below atmospheric pressure once the initial start-up phase has passed.

Carburettors

Some racers saw the Black Lightnings carburettors and quickly added TT carburettors to their steeds. If clip-fitting ones as per the Black Lightning were unavailable, they obtained flanged ones and soon fabricated flanged carburettor adaptors. Since the TT carburettors were originally intended for race machines, they had no real tickover adjustment, so when pressed into use on the road, a popular modification was to cut a small hole in the rear of the slide to enable a tickover to be maintained. By the early fifties GP carburettors also became available and even on misguided occasions Wal Philips fuel injectors were employed.

A TT carburettor shown installed on the front cylinder of a Grey Flash. The carburettor and inlet manifold are flanged in this picture, while the originals were clip fitting. The spark plug is also on the opposite side from standard. (Photo by Tim Kingham)

A Mikuni carburettor together with a suitable air filter. The special inlet manifold is available for the unit incorporating a matching sealing groove for the rubber moulded connector. (Photo by Angela Kingham)

As the old 289 carburettors on the Black Shadow wore out spares became difficult to locate. There was a move to modernise to the readily available Monoblocks as fitted to the Series 'D', or the later Amal Concentric design, while the more cosmopolitan owners tried Del-Autos. In the end the burgeoning classic bike industry realised the market potential and in the early seventies Burlen Ltd started to remanufacture the old designs of carburettors that had been superseded. Thus, over time, the old 276 and similar sizes were remanufactured; finally, with the urging of Vincent Spares, the range on offer included the special brass left-hand float chambered 229 front head version for the Shadow. Nowadays the biggest problem faced is the introduction of ethanol into petrol, especially in the UK where there is no other labelled option. Even the 5 per cent levels of ethanol cause a lot of trouble with fuel tanks, delivery systems, and carburettors. Many are the cures and replacement parts offered to ameliorate the problem. Sometimes even the slow running passages in the older carburettors are no longer the right size and need to be altered. The problems will only escalate with the planned increases in ethanol content in future years. Some riders have reasoned that fitting a carburettor, such as Mikuni carburettors that have been designed for the present day fuels, is a good solution, and although they may not look correct, in most cases they certainly perform flawlessly. Suitable carburettor adaptors for flange and Mikuni type carburettors are now available.

Exhaust System

The standard pipes are of 1⅝-inch diameter and are of Siamese construction. Perhaps surprisingly, the original Vincent pipe jigs are still in use. Other patterns of pipes have been tried, notably to avoid obstructing access to the timing cover, although none were really aesthetically pleasing. Regarding silencers, substitutes were available – some more successful than others – with the BSA Gold Star pattern being a popular choice with the sporting fraternity. Finally, in 2012, Vincent Spares and the VOC combined their efforts to recreate the original spiral silencer. For racing, the options were either the addition of a short pipe to the rear spindle instead of the silencer, or the full 2-inch twin pipes of the Black Lightning. One notable success in the sixties was Malcolm Elgar, who sprinted his Black Shadow in the road class. He rode to and won many events in the UK and the continent, utilising a 2-inch system that mimicked the lines of the standard system, including a 2-inch centre pipe absorption silencer.

Transmission

After 1955 it was soon noted that the Series 'D' had forty-four small springs in its engine shock absorber, rather than the thirty-six of the Series 'C'. This was introduced to help cure spring failures, which were a known fault caused perhaps by either a design error, or wear in the components. The Series 'D' shock absorber became the replacement choice of many. Recently, the VOC drawings committee has revisited the entire cam form and spring length.

As has been mentioned, the excellent Vincent clutch is not too tolerant of oil and needs careful assembly. Some owners also found the clutch improved if extra ventilation holes were drilled in the cover plate. A good improvement was obtained by fitting a needle roller thrust conversion, which helps to lift the clutch plate square. The lack of knowledge needed to adjust the clutch properly, the increasing wear, and the lack of component availability in the sixties suggested to many owners that the cure was to fit a multiplate clutch in its place. The earliest version comprised of a Norton clutch mounted on the original clutch shoe carrier. Later versions tended to use more sophisticated units from Japan's multi-cylinder 'super bikes', such as the Suzuki. However, one designed specifically for the Vincent was produced, called V2 or V4, depending on the manufacturer.

One of the problems associated with these clutches was the original design only needed to lift one plate, whereas it was now being asked to move a considerable distance more in order to separate many plates. Vincent Spares have produced a modified lever and adjuster, which fitted inside the gear box cover does make an increase in the lift available.

Above left: Variations of the engine shock absorber (ESA). On the left the Series 'D' design from 1955 on the right the original Series 'B'/'C'. (Photo courtesy of Vincent Spares)

Above right: A needle roller clutch conversion that enables the clutch plate to lift more squarely than with a single point pushrod. (Photo supplied by Norman Walker)

Right: Non-standard drillings in the clutch cover to help cool the internals. (Photo by Angela Kingham)

A view of the main components of a Norton clutch conversion. In the conversion pictured here the centre of the Norton clutch drum mounts onto the cut-down clutch shoe carrier, while the drum mounts in the same position as the original drum on a welded ring that contains the holes for the six standard bolts from the chain wheel. All the other components are standard Norton. (Photo by Tim Kingham)

The clutch adjuster modification comprises of a longer adjuster, which is fitted inside the gearbox cover and replaces the shorter standard (one also shown) that normally fits with a nut on the outside. The small adjustment in the lever position together with a revised operating arm increases the total available lift for a multiplate clutch. (Photo courtesy of Vincent Spares)

By far the most radical modification was the fitting of a Norton gearbox, since this required sawing off the back half of the crankcase to remove the gearbox casing. Often this was an occurrence in the late fifties, generally for racing, when crankcases were cheap and the art of setting up a Vincent box, or its parts, was in some localities a little lacking. In general, this also involved a Norton frame, or perhaps a racing sidecar chassis, although examples of Norton boxes in conjunction with a Vincent frame do exist. Finally, the best solution was realised when the late John Surtees in conjunction with Quaife produced a five-speed gear set, which fitted in the existing gearbox cavity as a straight swap. Those with an eye to detail could also source a modification to the gear cover to read not one to four digits, but one to five. Originally, the new set provided a different spaced bottom gear than standard, which some preferred, and nowadays two ratio choices are offered.

The size of the Vincent kick-start is a bit daunting and there is a technique to using it. Modifications to that instrument include a washer screwed onto the end of the spline to prevent it slipping, and doubling up on the internal ratchet spring. The biggest aid to starting came with the introduction of the electric start kit from François Grosset. The first thing to say is that he has achieved something many would have said was impossible, in that the starter is almost invisible and the kick-start is retained. This effect is obtained by a concentration on miniaturising the mechanisms that operate the starter motor, which in turn means the sprag clutch employed needs to be treated with care. Once again, for starting a strict technique is recommended, as a single transmitted backfire can shear the safety pin.

Another introduction by the racing fraternity was the use of ⅝-inch by ¼-inch chain rather than the ⅝-inch by ⅜-inch as standard. Racers and weight savers also employed alloy sprockets. Later, many have fitted an O-ring chain, which should be accompanied with an appropriate sprocket change as well.

That small bulge directly below the right-hand footrest and behind the exhaust pipe is all that can be seen of an electric start – and of course an extra button on the handlebar. (Photo by Bob Southall)

CHAPTER SEVEN

More Modifications

Frame and Suspension

As time went by the Vincent dampers started to leak; indeed the recommended service interval was only around 3,000 miles. Many were the schemes dreamt up to fill the damper's body with oil via the thoughtfully provided filler hole, while at the same time excluding the dreaded air bubbles that were want to hide in its cavities. The main problem was that the piston rod seal at the top of the damper always allowed a gradual seepage of oil and regular refilling seemed the only solution. As hydraulics improved into the mid-fifties, the ever-resourceful owners soon discovered an oil seal (used, it is believed, in a Jaguar car) and employed it in a modified housing in the top of the damper, thus improving things somewhat. Additional modifications included a one-way valve that allowed the oil to circulate through metered holes. A later suggestion was to pack part of the inner body space with bubble wrap. All these measures were aimed at reducing foaming in the body of the damper and loss of oil, although these were only palliative solutions, or solutions that retained the original damper. For those who desired good road holding and comfort over originality, what was really needed was a substitute damper. As noted earlier, the Series 'D' employed an Armstrong damper at the front and rear. The front Armstrong damper could be substituted onto the Series 'C'. Some Brampton forks were converted with a Woodhead Munroe unit, but the real breakthrough came in 1967 when Koni started to make motorcycle units and their dampers were introduced. Having been developed in the car world and designed to be hidden under tin skirts, they were finished in red oxide and were a little agricultural looking, but with a lick of silver paint on the body and black paint on the shroud they made a passable replica of the Vincent damper. They were adjustable and worked very efficiently. Their range of units was also increased when a damper for the Brampton was also offered. In 2000 Koni ended its motorcycle division and made a deal with an Australian firm who then produced shocks under the name Ikon (*see* below).

When Girdraulic forks became generally available, a lot of owners fitted them to machines with Brampton forks; indeed, the factory would do this retrofitting for you. Owners of a Series 'B' could cut the relevant UFM back tube to allow fitment of a rear damper; this further muddied the waters, which were already murky due to the slow introduction of Girdraulic by the factory during 1949–50. To complete the cycle some riders preferred the lightness and quickness of the Bramptons and thus fitted them in preference to Girdraulic type. The Bramptons can be further improved with a coil over damper, which are occasionally available and can be fitted without any major alteration. Stainless steel has also found a welcome place in the spindles of

Above left: View of a Koni damper that has been installed for many years. Also visible is the perennial problem of the concourse practitioner, scuffing on the chrome spring box inners by the outer covers. (Photo by Tim Kingham)

Above right: An adjustable Brampton coil over damper. This is a close up of the lower damper installation and shows one of the special clamping plates that avoids alteration of the original coil spring mount point on the fork. (Photo by Tim Kingham)

the Brampton and Girdraulic forks as corrosion, as much as wear on the plated steel spindles, served to reduce the efficiency of the suspension.

In the sixties Ken Pettiford developed the Pettiford spring, which he initially developed with touring and luggage equipment in mind. These were employed in the rear of the machine and were longer than standard, giving a degree of 'preload' when fitted, which enabled the whole bike to ride higher. A stiffer than standard version is available for sidecar use.

In the USA the Thornton suspension system offered either springs for Series 'C' and 'D' machines, or a complete system, which also included dampers to replace Koni or Vincent installations. It is claimed the springs were much softer than the original Vincent springs and have adjustable preload, while the dampers have a stage action and adjustable rebound action. Being an American firm means a legal liability release needs to be signed by the customer before any items can be purchased. They have also stated their lawyers forbade them to claim they were safer than the standard Vincent.

By 2010 the Australian Ikon dampers were available for Vincents, having an improved action from the old Koni dampers, with an appearance that is very close to the original Vincent damper. In 2014 a private initiative by a VOC member Rob Staley enabled the UK firm Avo to produce a range of Vincent dampers, including coil over dampers. As soon as dampers were available, especially after the example of the Series 'D' was to hand, there was an increase of owners fitting fully sprung seats. In practice

Only the lack of a brass filler plug indicates that this is an Ikon damper and not an original Vincent damper. (Photo courtesy of Vincent Spares)

The AVO damper shown is a coil over type for the rear; this renders the two separate spring boxes unnecessary. Other AVO dampers are available to just replace the standard front and rear damper units. (Photo by Rob Staley)

Fully sprung suspension is demonstrated here on No. 123 Reg Bolton's Twin. The tubular support continues from the normal rear seat fixing to the RFM pivot position, or footrest plate behind his right foot. No. 12 is the late Ian Hamilton on his special Vincent engine bike and No. 9 is Harvey Mitchell on a Comet – May 1987, Cadwell. (Photo Geoff Preece)

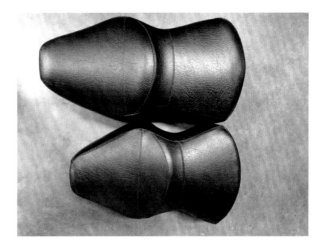

At the top is the 4-inch-longer model seat, below is the standard size seat. (Photo courtesy of Vincent Spares)

this consisted of removing the seat stays and supporting the seat on tubes from around the pillion footrest position. There was by consensus a definite improvement in the ride, providing a good damper was employed. The other improvement in comfort now available is the longer dual seat squab; obviously riders, or their passengers, must now be larger than those of 1948!

Steering and Speed Wobbles

The spectre that often stalks discussions on road holding is of the infamous Vincent speed wobble. Certain road undulations, an unused steering damper, tyres and their pressures have been implicated as a cause to this effect occurring. The wobble is not common nor is it confined to the Vincent, but is understandably traumatic and can result in injury to the rider if it happens. The two-piece steering damper as fitted to the Series 'D' is recommended and some riders fit hydraulic units. Another helpful modification is the replacement of the cup and cone head stock bearings with a taper roller kit. A lot of work is going on currently to improve the action of the forks under braking and the path the front wheel spindle takes as it operates. VOC members in the USA and the UK are experimenting with softer and progressive springs, different dampers, as well as modifications to the steering head, the eccentric position, and reduction of plain bearing 'sticking'. All these changes are being made with the aim of controlling and altering the forks movement. It is hoped eventually that this experimentation should result in an action more like that of a telescopic fork, or perhaps more appropriately that of a Brampton fork with a modern damper. The modifications also have the promise of improving road holding. These current modification exercises show that the tradition of improvement of the machine is still alive and ongoing.

Stands

The rear stand on the Series 'B' and 'C' was often regarded as an anachronism, but once the technique was mastered it was a very secure stand and many grew to love it. By the

Above left: A Kawasaki side stand fitted to the left-hand pillion footrest plate; the stop switch normally fitted to the Japanese bike has been removed. (Photo by Angela Kingham)

Above right: Dave Hills's centre stand fitted to a Series 'B' Rapide, the assembly comprises two new pillion footrest plates and is completed with a spring, pivot, and legs assembly. All the standard stands can be retained. (Photo supplied by Dave Hills)

sixties, what on many machines sealed its fate was the fad for abbreviated mudguards. When a shorter rear mudguard was employed, there was no flap left on which to secure the rear stand, so it was often removed and relegated to garage maintenance use or lost. The front stand arrangement faired much better as it was such a compact and useful design, but those Series 'B' owners retrofitting Series 'C' suspension soon found their front stands were too short. The same complaint occurred when Series 'C' owners raised their machines as they searched for improved suspension. One ingenious solution was to carry a wooden block on a string, on which to place the stand foot. On leaving astride the bike it would be brought upright and the block retrieved by the string! Since this stand assembly is not of inconsiderable weight, often circuit racing gave rise to the practice of removing completely the front cowl and stand assembly and then using a wall.

An alternative to the front stands was to use a single central prop stand from another machine, placing it somewhere in the region of the rear frame member pivot and pillion footrest plate on the left hand side. More recently this 'foreign' mid-prop stand is often encountered as an addition, making a surfeit of stands not an unusual occurrence. On the Series 'D' the lever operated stand was very efficient, if a little unsightly. It was only occasionally removed; generally this occurred on the open machines when the front Series 'C' stands were fitted. The real revolution came with the introduction of the Dave Hills tread down centre stand. These are available for Series 'B', 'C' and 'D' machines, and are tailored for the specific series and the wheel sizes of the machine on which it is to be fitted. It comprises of a stand, a pivot, and two side plates, which replace the two pillion footrest plates. Its attachment does not affect the existing standard stands and it is very easy to operate.

Wheels

The Black Lightning was equipped with 21-inch front and 20-inch rear alloy rims. While the diameter was not always copied, alloy rims in WM1 and WM2 were much in favour for the Black Shadows. A lot of tyres have been worn away since the initial tyres of the Black Shadows were specified and many and varied are those that have been fitted to the machine since. A criticism often made is the chain line prevents a wider tyre than 4 inches, or its metric equivalent to be used on the rear, especially on the Series 'B' models. What is often forgotten is by modern standards the machine has a modest power output. A wider tyre is probably not required, since increasing a tyre width also means increasing the rolling radius of the tyre, which in turn means forcing more lean for a given corner radius. Thus, it does not seem a big disadvantage to keep the rear tyres width to around its original size.

Although at the front 19- and 18-inch tyres have been used, there is an opinion the 20 x 3 inch still provides the stability and directional precision that suits the machine, especially on Brampton forks. The modern H rated 3 x 20 Avon Speed master is still available, but is rarely listed on Avon (Cooper Tyres) website. This occasionally results in bush fires of worry about obsolescence and short supply, leading to panic alteration by owners of the 20-inch wheel size to the more common 19 inch. This is unnecessary since, while not listed, the tooling for the 20-inch still survives. Batches of the 20 inch are made to the specific order of large suppliers, who distribute them to smaller outlets. The rear wheel being the more common 19-inch size has a number of alternatives available and again an Avon modern equivalent with a flat, or rounded profile is often recommended.

Brakes

Although the brakes were outstanding by the standards of 1948 and, when tested by *The Motor Cycle* in August 1949, a Black Shadow recorded a stopping distance of 26 feet 6 inches from 30 mph, the power of the bike meant that some still found them wanting in spite of this performance. One of the first pieces of received knowledge was to pull hard on the front brake and then tighten the wheel spindle, which would ensure that the shoes were centralised. Subsequent investigations by Trevor Southwell, noted in *MPH*, asserted the brake pivots were about 1 mm from their ideal position. Since this revelation occurred in the 1990s, the remedy of revising the brake shoes or moving the pivot was of only academic interest to most riders. It is possible a revision of the brake shoe dimensions may correct this error when new tooling is made.

A good practice adopted and still practiced today is to obtain the shoes with oversize linings, assemble them onto the brake plate, mount that on a lathe, and machine the linings to fit the drum. This obviates any error in the assembly.

A popular early modification was to braze a triangular support to the cam bearing on the outside to prevent flexing of the pillar under hard braking. When cast Black Lightning magnesium brake plates were available, a good solution was to fit these. Magnesium does have a propensity to corrode, so in the sixties aluminium copies started to appear, notably those from Roger Slater with cast in rather than separate attached air scoops. Today an improved version is available from Vincent Spares.

A steel brake plate modified probably for racing with a steel web to strengthen the brake pivot. An examination of a standard back wheel will reveal that the rear steel back plate brake pivot has an aluminium support as standard. One of the anchor pillars has been cut down, perhaps to save a few ounces, which renders the plate only useable on one side of the wheel. (Standard plates are not 'handed'- apart from the front speedometer hole.) There does not appear to be any rivet holes on the periphery of the plate that would allow attachment of a rain shield. (Photo by Tim Kingham)

Racing front brake plates in aluminium with provision for speedometer. These plates will fit Brampton forks as shown, or Girdraulic forks. The plates are to the pattern of the original Lightning magnesium ones. (Photo by Angela Kingham)

A braced aluminium shoe without a lining fitted. This is a recent development that includes a revised geometry in the relationship between shoe face and pivots. (Photo courtesy of Vincent Spares)

The actuation of the standard front brake was modified by the factory and is covered in Richardson's *Vincent Motor Cycle* in the true retrofit tradition. It describes the inclusion of a balance beam stop on the front fork bridge plate and details are given of a bracing plate to fit on the outside of the pivot, intended to reduce the bending motion of the pivot under hard braking. Discussion has ensued over the years about the effectiveness of the balance beam. Aside from beefing up the actuating cables, another modification was to install a balance compensator on the handlebar lever and anchor the twin cable ends with adjusters on stationary anchor points fixed to the forks. These were situated at about the same height instead of the balance beam. With regard to the shoes themselves, some racers have filled in the hollow in the shoe face before the cam and extended the lining to present more lining area. A recent development by Patrick Godet has produced shoes with increased webbing to support the lining face to prevent the flexure that contributes to the reduction in the brakes effectiveness.

Sometime in the early sixties Ferodo AM4 racing lining material became available and soon proved to be less prone to fade under frequent use. Those interested in braking under 'racing conditions' eagerly seized upon this lining. The disadvantage to the use of AM4 was the prevalence of a high-pitched squeal when braking hard. The only really bad side of this effect seemed to be the reported occasional vibration breakage of the brake shoe tension spring. Wise racers would entwine a loop of copper wire inside the spring between the shoe pegs to prevent it falling into the depths if the spring broke. The problem largely disappeared when the AM4 was outlawed because of its asbestos content.

The rear brake did not come in for a lot of modification. The aluminium copies of the Black Lightning rear brake plate could be fitted and it is possible to fit a second drum on a Series 'D', but generally when a big twin is down-shifting quickly and the rider is braking hard, there is not a lot of tyre adhesion left to exploit. Indeed, since it was not unknown for powerful motors to shear the cast-iron brake drum under fierce acceleration, for racing the drum was often removed from the sprocket side and substituted by an aluminium sprocket carrier. All the braking on the rear was then done on the single drum.

From the sixties and onwards, as the demands of the ever more congested roads increased, the resourceful Vincent owners were hard at work with regard to the front brake. After a spate of fitting 'foreign' drum brakes, the next big innovation came as disc brakes became generally available on contemporary motorcycles and the

One of the many variations of disc brakes fitted to Girdraulic forks, this one comprises twin discs. (Photo by Eddie Grew)

An 8-inch brake unit on the right with its matching 8-inch drum and on the left for comparison a standard 7-inch drum. (Photo courtesy of Vincent Spares)

A two-sided, two leading shoe brake plate with 30-mm-wide shoes, (Standard width: 23 mm or 7/8 inch). It is also supplied with a new hollow axle. (Photo by Vincent Speet)

opportunity to fit disc brakes was now viable. It proved relatively easy for an inventive owner to fit single or twin disc brakes to a set of Girdraulic forks. The consensus of opinion seemed to indicate given the relative small footprint of a 20-inch tyre, a single disk at the front was sufficient. The trend now is for small batch production of 7- or 8-inch diameter, single or double leading shoe front brakes that mirror as far as possible the external design forms of the original.

Electrics

Many alternative headlamp light units have been tried; Marchal and Cibie are some more exotic units that shared upgrades with the more prosaic Lucas pre-focus units in the Series 'C' headlamp shell.

The rise of LED lighting continues to encroach on the territory of filament bulbs and a reasonably priced and effective headlight unit is almost with us. The first real installation of the LED on Vincents came with an up-rating of the STOP lamp, so beloved of Vincent owners. There is a conversion widely available that features a dense cluster of LED, making it a practical light. The installation of this conversion means the previous modification of fitting a Lucas 564, or similar lens as mentioned earlier, was itself superseded as new 'old' stop lights were refitted. Such are the changes effected by the changing demands of fashion, originality and utility.

Direction indicators are also almost an essential nowadays as many car drivers have no idea about hand signal meanings. LED technology has helpfully enabled the manufacture of small units that are inconspicuous in installation, but very obvious when activated.

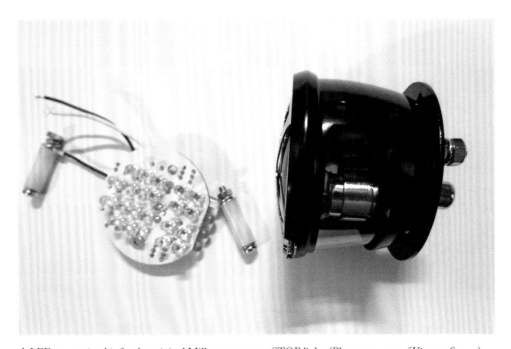

A LED conversion kit for the original Miller pattern rear STOP light. (Photo courtesy of Vincent Spares)

The Lucas dynamo and regulator being the choice for the Series 'D' was a retrofit option for the Series 'C'. Those retrofitting 3-inch dynamos of any type to the early Series 'B' crankcases, originally intended for 3.5-inch units, needed to fit a spacer in their cast cradles. *MPH* and *Know Thy Beast* gave details of how, with a little internal alteration of the wiring, it was possible to up-rate the 6-volt dynamo to 12 volt. This placed an increased strain on the unit and suppliers came with an updated solid-state regulator that replaced the electro mechanical devices, but could be fitted inside their metal housings or fibreglass replicas. In the USA the late John McDougal produced a

Left: The Walkernator is a compact car alternator driven by a countershaft and belt from the dynamo position and it provides more than enough power to supply all lighting needs, winkers and electric clothing etc. An auxiliary cover can be placed over the end if required to present a clean appearance. (Photo by Norman Walker)

Below: A modified primary drive with an additional housing to house a Lucas alternator, in this instance it is fitted on an Egli with a left-hand exhaust pipe. (Courtesy of BSK Speedworks)

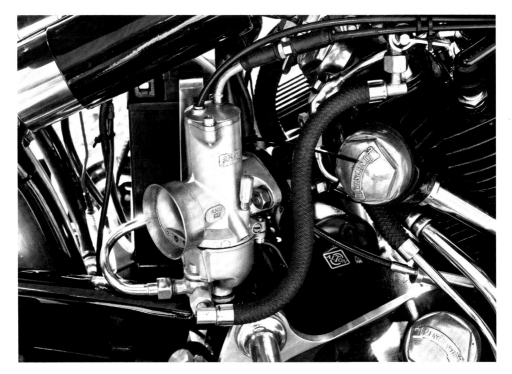

Occupying the same footprint as the original Miller or Lucas dynamo, this is an Alton generator. Also visible is a very neat concentric carburettor installation. (Photo by Bob Southall)

12-volt 'McDougulator' from a Kubota tractor alternator, which could be fitted in the twin. In the UK Norman Walker produced the 'Walkernator' alternator conversion based on an alternator from a Citroen 2CV. There were also attempts to fit a Lucas RM12 alternator and its successors on the crank, a not unexpected modification because this method has been the standard ware on parallel twins since around 1953. Many felt the alternator conversion was unsightly. This objection does not apply to one alternative, which is the 12-volt Alton generator produced by Paul Hamon. This French offering is an alternator and regulator system, which fits easily into the original cradle and looks like the original Lucas or Miller items.

Even before the Series 'D' came with coil ignition fitted, attempts had been made to fit coil ignition instead of a magneto. There were good reasons for this, centring mainly on easy replacement of parts and repairs in remote areas. An additional advantage was the reduction of loads on the driving pinion. There was also the ease of fitting a rev counter to be considered, since on a magneto this involved either fitting a drive that allowed the ATD mechanism to still work, or necessitated the fitting of a manual end cap to the magneto body.

For coil ignition, initially a distributor body from other machines was employed, many fitting a D twin cylinder type cam. Some managed to squeeze two modified contact breakers into the distributor head to closely control the individual cylinder break points. As the ignition technology improved, proprietary units started to come onto the market, notably Pazon and Boyer Bransden. These utilise a programmed ignition curve, while there was also the Grosset system with mechanical advance.

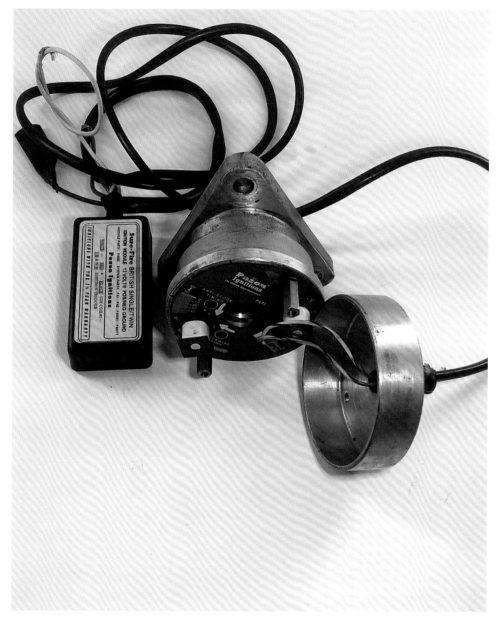

A Pazon coil ignition installation ready to be fitted in the magneto position. The 'black box' and coil (coil not shown) can be installed remotely from the ignition unit. (Photo by Tim Kingham)

Finally, Tony Harris created a very clever solution; he revived an old English magneto name BT-H and, after a lot of development, produced a superb BT-H electronic magneto, which in 2002 was placed on the market with versions that included Vincent singles and twins. As well as providing an electronic advance curve, the unit fits snugly under the magneto cowl and, best of all, it provides a neat locking method. This involves placing a rod through the unit rotor to lock the rotation while the engine is

A BT-H installation, the electronic unit occupies the standard magneto position while the associated coils mounted below are small enough to also fit under the front cowl. (The front cowl has been removed for this picture). (Photo by Angela Kingham)

timed, meaning that the struggle to stop the magneto or distributor spindle slipping when securing the taper nut has been eliminated.

Finish

There were a few attempts to paint the Vincent blue or red – perhaps in emulation of the factories occasional lapses into colour – but generally the black finish remained. Some Rapide engines were painted black as they were 'Shadowised'. No doubt influenced by a trickle of information emanating from the USA, in the early sixties there was a phase of stripping the paint from Girdraulics, polishing the legs, and heavily chroming many parts of the machine. In this regard it should not be forgotten that the factory itself had been guilty of a few chromium tanks for export. The 'Glam' fad has long passed and the excess chrome has mostly been returned to a staid black again. The only permanent change to the finish was, and is, the extension of a feature present on the original machines of the use of stainless steel. Many parts, including all the fixings and fastenings that were originally cadmium plated steel, and after thirty or forty years were showing their age, are now produced in stainless steel. Current electroplating regulations mean it's a resourceful and dedicated restorer who is able to source cadmium plating nowadays, or indeed find normal steel items to plate. As a matter

An example of weight saving: a large cap for the oil filter chamber, which is normally a brass machined casting, but which here has been made in aluminium to save weight. A standard tool kit K1 spanner is shown undoing it. (Photo courtesy of Marcus Bowden)

of interest, it was the provision of stainless steel fastenings that formed one of the mainstays of the early VOC club shop. At the same time, the racer orientated owners, bent on reducing weight to a minimum, diligently followed a course of replacing many of those same steel items and anything else possible with aluminium.

Finally, it must be emphasized that Vincent owners themselves, through seventy years of experience with their machines, initially devised most, if not all, of these modifications. Many of these modifications have been taken up by Vincent Spares and other suppliers and are available today.

CHAPTER EIGHT

The Successors

Production Figures

It is difficult to be precise on the number of twins made during the Vincent production years. Towards the end of production the remaining records are poor, but the VOC Machine Registrar and Machine Researcher continue to fill in the blanks. There are a remaining 107 machines that were made, which are not even specified as a twin, or a single, although a good estimate based on the VOC records as of late 2016 are:

Series 'B' Black Shadows – 77
Series 'C' Black Shadows – 1,568 including 15 white shadows
Series 'D' Black Shadows – 145
Total 1,790

The total of 1,790 Shadows compares to a Rapide total of 4,829, thus claims that Black Shadow production exceeded that of the Rapide it seems are 'greatly exaggerated'. A total of around 6,900 post-war motorcycles produced by Vincents were twins, which included Black Shadows, Black Lightnings, Rapides, Black Knights and the 115 or so successors to the Black Shadow, the Black Prince. If one includes the singles – the Comet, Meteor, and the Grey Flash – there were around 11,037 complete Vincents made and almost 40 per cent remain on record with the VOC.

Spares Continue

The last machine from the Vincent factory bearing the name Black Shadow was produced in late 1955. The last big twin was its short-lived successor, a Black Prince, which was completed just before Christmas 1955. After the Vincent motorcycle production finished, the Vincent Company continued to manufacture other products, including the Firefly moped, an early water scooter the Amanda, and a small two-stroke engine with its related products, but more importantly they maintained a spares supply for the motorcycles and a service facility.

Finally, and perhaps inevitably, in late 1959 the Vincent business in Stevenage was sold to Harpers Engineering and PCV left to start a garage business – a venture that proved to be short-lived. Harpers continued with the spares supply and by 1960 they were offering rebuilt Rapides. These were stated as being completely refurbished from existing bikes and they continued at a low level of production into the sixties. There was, however, a quoted delivery time of a year, with a price tag of over £350. It is also unlikely that any of these at that time were built to Black Shadow specification.

In 1964 *Motorcycle Mechanics* carried out a road test of a Harpers rebuilt Black Shadow and reportedly obtained 124 mph and a 22 foot stopping distance from 30 mph. Pictures at the time show that its specification did not include a 5-inch speedometer.

False Dawns and Decline

In the years that followed the closure there were many attempts to remanufacture a modern Vincent. Although the concept of 'modern' may have changed, it is a process that continues to this day. The twin engine has been fitted to many frames – Norton, Vincent frames with tele forks and swinging arms, and often-unique custom-built frames. Many of these creations were private one offs and a few were more ambitious and did reach small production levels. Most were content to append the short form of the Vincent name as a 'Vin' (as in Norvin) to their creations, or the full Vincent name as a suffix e.g.: The Parkin Vincent, the Curtis Vincent, and of course the Egli Vincent. Except insomuch as they served to boost spares use, and occasionally absorbed a Black Shadow engine, these machines are really peripheral to the Black Shadow story. In the interests of clarity, however, there were at least two major attempts where machine creators felt they needed to use derivations of the Black Shadow name. In 1970 Roger Slater moved on to produce his own Egli frames under licence and offered two complete bikes – the Rapide and the Shadow 70. Production ran for around three years and it is unlikely that the Shadow 70 production exceeded double figures. In 1994 Bernard Li, an American millionaire, wanted to develop a new Vincent. He intended to use the Vincent name and fit a Honda RC51 V twin or another V twin power plant. In spite of being quoted by the press, as in the spirit of the Black Shadow, it was really never going to be another Black Shadow, but more an American Harley Davidson-type cruiser. Black Lightning and Black Eagle were names floated and a few prototypes were built, but sadly Bernard Li was killed in a motorcycle accident in Arizona, thus ending another dream that sought to capitalise on the Black Shadow legend.

Returning to Harpers, the direct successors to the Vincent Company, in 1965 Cope Allman International acquired the Harper group, which included Harper Engines. In the autumn of 1966 it was announced they had been investigating the possibility of starting Vincent production again. It was not just an idle thought as they appointed a Mr Coyston to start an investigation, which included a visit to the TT and the handing out of lots of questionnaires. Following that activity, a meeting was convened with the great and the good of the then current VOC, who drew up a specification of the Series 'E'. The specification was published in *MPH* and even today with the passing of sixty years, its 'GT' specification, while retaining the basic Vincent concept, stands the test of time. This is a feat that deserves recognition and is best appreciated if one tries to imagine a group of riders in 1900 imagining anything near the specification of a 1960 motorcycle! To complete the investigation a questionnaire was included in the October 1966 *MPH* for completion by the members – echoing the Series 'D' survey! Alas, it all came to nothing.

Around the middle of 1966, the club started to crystallise its ideas about spares. This followed an unofficial statement by Harpers that the comprehensive list of spares would start to shorten, as some parts were dropped as they became 'uneconomic to make'. The club decided to create a position for a spares officer, who would be a member of the executive committee and would hopefully recruit helpers. By April of the following year the shop was selling stainless steel fasteners for the covers of all machines and the list of items supplied started to lengthen.

The club shop was slowly gaining products, but it was still a voluntary exercise and by late 1970 the official position was that, while the club had decided not to compete with products supplied by Harpers, they were prepared to supply parts, which had a reasonable demand. Apart from Harpers' retail side, there were a number of small companies retailing Vincent spares; notable among them were Russell Motors, who later sold out to Mellor motors, Millars Motors, The Jolly Thresher Garage, Deeprose Bros, W. E. Humphreys, and Conway Motors.

A New Start

By 1974 it was obvious that the spares situation was becoming critical. At the beginning of 1975 Cope Alman started to divest Harper Engines of its interests. As the situation regarding Vincent spares remained unclear, the club entered into negotiations with Harpers to purchase the business, but then on 12 May 1975 it was announced that Matt Holder had bought the Vincent business. This was not an unexpected outcome as he held rights to manufacture spares for a number of makes from the old British motorcycle industry, such as Scott and Velocette – plus he had a good hold on supplies for Royal Enfield. Given the situation, and not sure of the ongoing spares availability and what exactly was going to be supplied in the future, the then VOC secretary Brian Harding had already taken action. Together with, Fred Rossiter and David Greaves, and aided by the rest of the VOC Executive, they had made contingency plans, which resulted in the formation of the VOC Spares Company Ltd (Vincent Spares). This was financed by purchases of share certificates by club members, motorcycle clubs, and individual members of the public. Matt Holder then agreed to cooperate with Vincent Spares as a major supplier and parts initially were only sold to the existing dealers. David Greaves and his wife Jane closed the Jolly Thresher Garage and became the first employees running the new Vincent Spares Company from their site in Lymn, Cheshire.

Over the next ten to fifteen years the spares situation started to improve and the retail model with the old spares distributors tended to disappear. By 1990 the remaining distributors were more engineering based producers, like T. W. Maughan & Sons, Furness & Searle, Bob Culver, and Bob Dunn, who offered rebuilds and engineering work. A number of other suppliers, while still retaining a retail function, were also initiating products and supplies. Notably among those were Ron Kemp and Conway Motors. Vincent Spares was also now in the retail business selling direct to customers, as well as organising much of the spares supply.

The Drawing Project

By the mid-1990s it was apparent to those who knew about such things that, although Vincent Spares was carrying out the basic task of organising the supply of spares, many of the components were not being produced to the correct dimensions. A lot of the commissioning of replacements was by other suppliers and thus not in the control of Vincent Spares, or more importantly could not be confirmed as being to the correct dimensions. Negotiations were made with Mr Holder with a view to obtaining the original drawings, but these were not successful, so it became clear some other action had to be taken. Initially, back at the start of the Vincent Spares Company, Phil Irving had donated a number of drawings, and now Bob Culver donated quite a lot more original drawings. These drawings were then used as a basis to improve the accuracy of components. In many ways this course of redrawing was the correct one, bearing in mind that the available drawings were by then around forty or fifty years old, their physical state was poor, and in some cases the accuracy of the materials they referred to was such that it was imperative that new drawings were created, and thus 'the gang of six' became the VOC drawings committee.[12] Such is the enormity of the task that although personnel have changed over the years, it is still in action over twenty years later.

The Very, Very Last Shadow

By mid-2004 the work of the Drawing Committee and the Vincent Spares Company had reached the point where it was feasible to produce an entire Black Shadow engine. This possibility was realised in what was called the 'engine project' and its championship by the VOC. The then managing director of Vincent Spares, David

The VOC/Vincent Spares Black Shadow engine project. The carburettors were set at extremely weak settings in order to scrape through the VOSA test. (Picture courtesy of the Vincent HRD Owners Club)

Meadowcroft, enabled the last few engine components to be produced to drawing and to the correct standard. Notably among the items thus created were the rear cylinder head casting and a full flywheel assembly. The project had great success in powering the general availability of those long-term unavailable and expensive items. The project team then went looking for a frame in which to test the finished engine. Luckily, the then VOC chairman, Tim Kirker, was halfway through a rebuild of his own machine and so it temporarily became a Black Shadow, and in early July 2005 it started its test mileage.

After this project was successfully completed, the obvious question then arose as to the viability of building a complete bike – hoping that in doing so, it would have the same effect on the cycle parts availability as the engine project had done with its own parts. It was agreed that the VOC would place the order for a Black Shadow with the Vincent Spares Company and finance the project. Thus, the very last Black Shadow was to be built.

Again a number of items needed to be sourced. The major items needed were the UFM (oil tank) fabrication, the RFM, the Girdraulic fork blades, and the top link. Of these items the fork blades posed the biggest problem, since originally these were aluminium forgings made in large batches by Thos. Smith's Stampings, Coventry. Obviously, changes to technology, availability, and cost made that method an impossible task. However, modern technology provided an answer; the Birmingham University Department of Metallurgy supplied the metal specification and the blades were

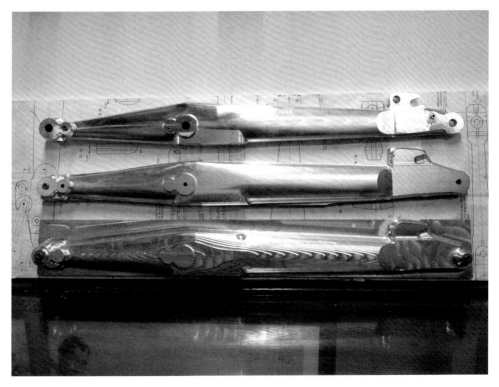

A display of the stages of CAD machining of the Girdraulic fork leg. This was done from a special billet of alloy. (Photo courtesy of Vincent Spares)

CNC machined from a blank to a finish that made them practically indistinguishable from the originals, yet with significantly improved strength.

Glyn Johnson assembled the parts and the machine was started just at the end of 2006. In early 2007 the last Black Shadow was complete and was handed over to the VOC. Soon it was on display at the Bristol Classic show to great acclaim, but by March it faced the difficult VOSA test to comply with the modern UK bike construction regulations that were current at the time. After some head scratching and remedial work (e.g. addition of mirrors and indicators) it passed and the jubilation that followed increased when the DVLA decided to issue it with a brand new 07 number (and not a Q plate). By May it was on the road and the VOC information officer Paul Adams planned a busy schedule of shows and publicity. These included tests by many of the motorcycle classic magazines, but to the delight of all, the weekly paper *Motor Cycle News* published an extremely complimentary test after the green leather-clad tester cornered at speeds very seldom seen before or since on Vincents.

In June it was offered for sale to members via a bidding form included in *MPH*. An announcement of the winner was planned for October 2007, but in the end member's bids did not reach the reserve. The Black Shadow was subsequently offered for sale at Bonham's Auction in the late April of 2008, when it sold for £34,500, which equates to £30,000 after buyer premium. Amazingly, this was less than the market value at the time of a good second-hand original. The sale price was enough to recoup the

The last Black Shadow on show after completion in 2007, sixty years after the first prototype was built. (Picture courtesy of the Vincent HRD Owners Club)

A riders' view of the new Shadow. (Picture courtesy of the Vincent HRD Owners Club)

The last Black Shadow on display in New Zealand's Nelson Museum before its move to Invercargill. (Photo by Tony Milbourn)

costs of the exercise and that was without allowing for the shot in the arm for the spares supply that its manufacture created. It eventually went to New Zealand, first to the Nelson-based NZ Classic Motorcycles, and then Transport World for the Classic Motorcycle Mecca collection in Invercargill, where it now resides. While the odometer on it still only registers under 1,000 miles, it was indeed a remarkable effort by the VOC and the Vincent Spares Company.

Today

In mid-2009, after changes in managing directors, Vincent Spares moved to Kettering. Under the managing director Ian Savage, Vincent Spares has made great progress in developing the customer base, adding a new computer online ordering system and website. The company now has two full and two part-time employees. It has moved into a position where the profits now made can be reinvested into renewing tooling, spares, making possible projects, (like the remanufacture of the Vincent spiral silencer), and restocking with those slow-moving expensive items, such as fork legs and oil tanks. It also has championed the sale of member's motorcycles at the company's premises and in doing so is happy to give a fair appraisal of the bikes condition and asking price.

The Future

Time marches on and this has consequences for the future of the Vincent. Parts wear out and corrosion occurs, replacement parts are made in smaller batches and costs increase. On the human side, the pool of original detailed Vincent knowledge reduces as experts retire or sadly die. There are mitigating factors, machining technology and materials constantly improve and become more available. Parts are more durable and accurate and with reduced set up times components can be produced economically in smaller batches; in fact there is already one component that is made by 3D printing. Regarding the loss of knowledge, the existence of a good pool of correct drawings that can be adhered to and good records are a great advantage. Accurate components may not always mean a trouble-free assembly, as parts that were made after the factory closed and before the Vincent Spares got into production were sometimes made in the absence of drawings by copying a 'good original'. In addition it should not be forgotten that even the original factory also had significant accuracy problems in their nine years of production. This situation can then lead to complaints that the new item made to drawing does not fit, when the fault is actually in the item it is being fitted to, so it would seem a good fitter with the requisite skills is still required. Nowadays, in the information age, there is a greater exchange and repository of knowledge about the Vincent than ever before, but the best advice is still to join the VOC, where as a member you will benefit from the other members experience and knowledge. Joining is also a sensible option for collectors, as well as riders, because the club registrar has access to many of the original build sheets, which confirm what is and what is not, an original machine.

Drive side of a lightly modernised 1952 Black Shadow. Wherever possible cadmium plating has been retained. The bike has 12-volt lighting, electric start, and electronic ignition. (Photo by Bob Southall)

There is no doubt that the lifetime of a Vincent and in particular the Black Shadow has far exceeded the designer's original expectations. They are one of the few mid-twentieth century vehicles still quite capable of keeping up with modern traffic and it is likely that they could continue to be in working condition for decades yet. What is not so likely is they will be used as the designer intended. It is an observable fact for a spares supply to be maintained and the spares to remain a viable business, the machines need to be used and continue to wear out those spares. Restoring a Vincent to replicate exactly a machine that left the factory seventy odd years ago is certainly possible, but the owner may then feel it is purely an investment, and he may subsequently doubt the machine can be used in that condition for regular reasonable journeys on modern roads. Certainly, such fears, unsubstantiated or not, will fuel the rise of the collector and fill the museums halls.

What is also debatable is the government's future attitude to their use on public roads. The changes to fuel content, the rise of the self-driving car, the attitude of the environmental lobby, the trend towards shared ownership of individual transport, ignorance, and indifference about our engineering heritage all may lead to a perfect

Timing side of the Black Shadow with a Satnav mounted. The wiring exists for indicators, but they are not fitted. Restoration took three years and was completed early 2016. It is a bike to be ridden and admired. (Photo by Bob Southall)

storm, where a minorities rights could be overturned and the removal of historic vehicles from the public roads might become a possibility. On the other hand, like steam railways and horse riding, which enhance our leisure time and our tourist industries, we could enter a golden age of enjoyment of our historic vehicles. If that occurs, at the forefront will undoubtedly be the legendary Vincent Black Shadow.

Second-hand Prices for the Black Shadow and Rapide – 1956 to 2016

Methodology and Results

Prices were collected on a year-by-year basis, picking advertised prices throughout each calendar year. Throughout the sixty years, only manufactured post-war Series 'C' machines were sampled. No Series 'A' or 'D', no basket cases, specials, Egli, or sidecar outfits were included. Also excluded were machines not offered in pounds sterling and none that did not specify a model name. Obviously condition of bikes, sellers' expectations, and time of year vary. To accommodate this variation the mean value for each year for each type was calculated and not the average, and this helped to offset especially high or low sales or expectations or those of special provenance. Those with 'offers starting at' were entered at that starting price.

The selling habits and methods have changed over sixty years, so the data was collected from various sources. Back in 1956 most adverts were trade with only occasional private entries, and all adverts were in *The Motor Cycle* or *Motorcycling*; in the first five years or so adverts were numerous and random selections were made from early spring, high summer, and autumn. This pattern continued into the sixties until the magazines themselves altered or ended. Private adverts in *Motor Cycle News* gained the ascendancy slowly and trade entries were no longer present or used. By the seventies all entries were declining (lower numbers mean poorer accuracy), so all the entries for a year were included in the calculation. As the eighties came the new classic bike magazines started and they became the avenue of choice for adverts, but entries were still low and by the later eighties were becoming sparse so *MPH* adverts were then included, a practice which continued to the end of the survey. By the millennium the forces of eBay and the Internet started to be felt, and by 2003 auction results were also included in the data set. It should be remembered that until then all the prices were asking prices and not true sales prices.

The results consist of two graphs. One shows the actual mean of the price value, which is interesting but not very comparable, while the second shows the mean price expressed in present-day terms by multiplying the mean price as it was in that year by the increase due to inflation from that year until autumn 2016, using the RPI index. To illustrate this point the last new offered prices that could be found advertised are from April 1956 and are for an open Series 'D' Rapide and an open Series 'D' Black Shadow, where the Rapide was £334 and Shadow was £365.[13] This equates today as a Rapide worth £7,915 and Black Shadow worth £8,650. As a comparison from the same source, a new Series 'D' Black Knight's and Series 'D' Black Prince's prices were £359 and £390 – £8,508 and £9,243 respectively.[14]

You will note that the inflation-adjusted graph shows more effectively the variations in prices year by year, but of course as it gets nearer the present day the inflation effect reduces and it closely matches actual prices. A couple of other interesting points are that the particular manufacturing year of a bike soon ceased to have much effect on price while its condition obviously does, and it was a couple of decades after 1956 before there was any real noticeable price gap between Rapides and Shadows.

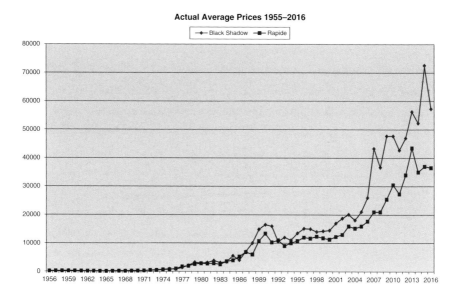

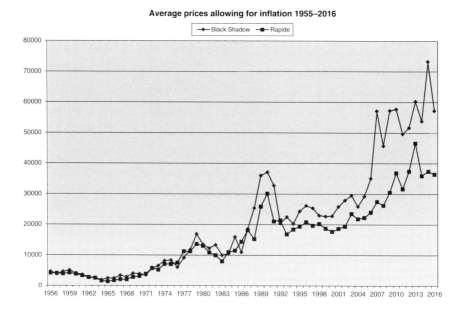

Footnotes

[1] Factory number two was acquired at the end of the Second World War and was known as the 'Fisher Green Works'. Harpers later used part of the site to sell spares, the buildings were demolished in 1980 and its site was occupied by a building called 'Vincent Court'.

[2] Jim Sugg managed the road test department. A new bike would take about half a day to be checked, adjusted, fitted with slave exhausts etc. and taken for a test run on the public roads by one of the testers. About a hundred miles was an average testing distance.

[3] With regard to the initial low production figures, the VOC Machine Registrar confirmed these from the factory records.

[4] This was patented by PCV on 15 February 1927. It was titled 'Improvements in or Relating to Spring Frames for the Driving Wheels of Cycles, Motorcycles and the like Vehicles'. After acceptance it was given the patent number 290735.

[5] Vincent used Pinchin & Johnson undercoat and Black Stoving enamel, the same as the renowned pre-war Marston Sunbeam motorcycles.

[6] Some early specifications seem to indicate the ends of the barrel fins were polished.

[7] The Girdraulic fork was first tested on *Gunga Din*, on Harold Taylors sidecar outfit in the 1948 ISDT, and the works commercial sidecar float. They were deemed ready for release to coincide with the 1948 Motorcycle Show.

[8] Classic Bike December 'for the record' 1992 Vic Willougby. MPH No. 314 March 1975 – 'One Man's Memories'- Ted Davis. MPH No. 526 Jan 1993 – 'The Montlhery Attempt', MPH No. 530 March 1993. 'The Last day at Montlhery', Jack Lazenby letter to Classic Bike 1993.

[9] Although Lightnings were mentioned in a number of accounts, the VOC Machine Registrar Simon Dinsdale has examined the factory records and it seems that no Lightnings were available at that point in the year (only three were built that year anyway). It would seem (again from the records) there were five Black Shadows built for the attempt, of which two or three were most probably in full Lightning trim to be used for the abortive 'short duration records', and two or three were specifically for the twenty-four hour attempt. The reason for the lack of precision is one of the machines was a 'hack' bike for test runs and press photos (subsequently broken for a Norvin in the sixties) and one has no build sheet available. In this day and age when numbers seem so important, it is worth noting they were all stamped as Black Shadows and later sold as such. It is almost certain that *Gunga Din* was also present.

[10] 100,000 miles in a year is a constant average speed of over 11 mph!

[11] The Vincent Owners Club Spares Company Ltd (VOCSC) trading as Vincent Spares.

[12] The 'gang of six' in February 1966 comprised Dave Hills (chairman), Frank Griffin (draftsman) John Coates, John Sayer, Bob Culver and Derek Sayer. (Neville Higgins and George Spence were also involved.)

[13] It would have taken the average earner in 1956 around eight months' wages to buy a new Black Shadow.

[14] The 'new' RPI calculated prices for 1955–56 are relatively low compared to the price of a new motorcycle of today, which is due in part to the fact the RPI inflation figure is calculated for all items, not just inflation prone manufactured ones.

Bibliography

Bickerstaff, J. P., *Original Vincent Motorcycle*, Bay View Books, Bideford Devon UK (1997)

Carrick, Peter, *Vincent-HRD*, Patrick Stephens Ltd, Cambridge UK (1982)

Clark, R. M., *Vincent Gold Portfolio* (compendium), Brooklands Books, Chobham UK (1980)

Harper, Roy, *The Vincent HRD Story*, Vincent Publishing Co., Spalding (1975)

Harper, Roy, *The Snarling Beast (PCV anthology)*, Vincent Publishing Co., Spalding (1979)

Irving, P. E., *Tuning for Speed*, Temple Press Books, London (1948)

Irving, Phil, *Motorcycle Technicalities*, Turton & Armstrong, Sydney Australia (1983)

Irving, Phil, *Rich Mixture*, Vincent Publishing Co., Spalding (1976)

Main-Smith, Brice, *Vincent-HRD Motorcycles* (new edition), BMS & Co., Leatherhead (1973)

Preece, Geoff, *A Photographic Miscellany*, VOC, Halifax (1999)

Richardson, Paul, *Vincent Motorcycles*, C. Arthur Pearson, London (1955)

Stevens, E. M. G., *Know Thy Beast*, Vincent-HRD Owners Club, UK (1972)

Vincent, P. C., *PCV – An Autobiography*, Vincent Publishing Co., Spalding (1976)

Wright, David, *Vincent – The Complete Story*, Crowood Press Ltd, Basingstoke (2002)

Wright, David, *Vincent-HRD and the Isle of Man*, Amulree Publications, Laxley IOM (1998)

Wright, David, *Vincent-HRD – How They Were Promoted and Sold*, Amulree Publications, Laxley IOM (2005)

Periodicals

Motorcycle Mechanics, Mercury House Publications, London (1959–83)

Motorcycle News, Bauer Consumer Media, Peterborough (1955–on)

Motorcycling, Mortons Media, Horncastle (1943–1967)

MPH – The Monthly Club Magazine of the VOC, Vincent Owners Club, UK (1948–on)

The Classic Bike, Mortons Media, Horncastle (1978–on)

The Classic Motorcycle, Mortons Media, London (1981–on)

The Motorcycle, Mortons Media, Horncastle (1943–67)